Adulting
Made Easy

Get Creative 6
An imprint of Mixed Media Resources LLC
19 West 21st Street, Suite 601, New York, NY 10010
SixthandSpringBooks.com

Editor **Pamela Wissman**
Art Director **Irene Ledwith**
Designer **Danita Albert**
Chief Executive Officer **Caroline Kilmer**
President **Art Joinnides**
Chairman **Jay Stein**

Cover and interior illustrations © Ruby Taylor

Library of Congress Cataloging-in-Publication Data
Names: Morin, Amanda, author.
Title: Adulting made easy : things someone should have told you about getting your grown-up act together / Amanda Morin.
Description: First edition. | New York, NY : Get Creative 6, [2021] | Includes index.
Identifiers: LCCN 2020039457 | ISBN 9781684620210 (paperback)
Subjects: LCSH: Young adults--Life skills guides. | Young adults--Finance, Personal. | Young adults--Conduct of life. | Adulthood.
Classification: LCC HQ799.5 .M67 2021 | DDC 646.70084/2--dc23
LC record available at https://lccn.loc.gov/2020039457

Manufactured in China

7 9 10 8 6

First Edition

Adulting Made Easy

Things Someone Should Have Told You About Getting Your Grown-Up Act Together

Amanda Morin

 Get Creative 6

Contents

Chapter 1
As an adult, you decide how to spend your money, but you're also accountable for the consequences. This chapter covers what expenses you can expect to have, how to budget for them, and strategies for avoiding costly mistakes.

Chapter 2
A steady income is how you'll get to do adult things and be able to pay the bills adults pay. This chapter covers looking for jobs, applying for jobs, job interviews, accepting a job offer, avoiding mistakes, and asking for a raise.

Chapter 3
Being an adult means communicating in many situations and speaking up for yourself. This chapter covers conversation skills, apologies, keeping in touch, and more.

Chapter 4
You've probably used social media most of your life to connect with people and share things, but it's also easy to make mistakes. This chapter covers its rewards and consequences, thinking before you post, and your online reputation.

Chapter 5
Being an adult is also about being a good citizen while taking advantage of your rights and privileges. This chapter covers getting a driver's license or state ID, voting, changing your address, and protecting your identity.

Introduction

"Adulting is hard." How many times have you seen this as a hashtag, a lament, or a meme on a social media feed? If the answer is never, I'm going to assume you don't use social media. The rest of us, though, have seen it. In fact, as I write this, I'm drinking from a cup with "Adulting is Hard" on it. Since I just spilled coffee all over my last clean, ironed, work-appropriate shirt from that cup, I'm inclined to agree. Adulting can be hard. I know—I've been adulting for a while now. But it doesn't have to be!

As of the writing of this book, I've also successfully raised two children to adulthood and am still working on raising a third. Keep in mind, that's not the same thing as raising them to be successful adults. The jury's still out on that. All it means is that I did the best I could to make sure they have the skills they need to be out in the so-called real world.

But I didn't write this because I did such a good job raising adults. And I'm definitely not writing it because I'm so good at adulting. The truth is, when I first hit adulthood, I was terrible at it. So terrible at it that it should—and will—serve as a cautionary tale to you.

Looking Back

I got married young the first time. I was nineteen years old. And, yes, I did say "the first time." I've been married twice. The second marriage has stuck, in no small part due to the fact that I've been much better at adulting this time around. I also had my first child a month before my twenty-second birthday. I was all in for adulting at a young age.

But in my late teens and early twenties, I had no idea how to budget well and didn't think to buy what I needed to make or clean an actual home. My first apartment was conveniently located next to a fast-food chain that will not be named, but that had apple pies, hamburgers, and french fries on a two-for-a-dollar menu. Suffice to say, we spent more money than we could afford on fast food. I gained forty pounds in a very short period of time, and used the sink and stove in my small apartment as storage space for non-cookware-related items that I tended to buy while impulse shopping.

And then I smartened up. Just kidding. I didn't. After finishing college, I got my first professional job as a kindergarten teacher and was thrilled to be making a whopping $18,000 per year. It didn't occur to me that I'd have to start paying back student loans once I got a job, nor were the implications of consolidating my student loans with those of my first husband clear to me. Also, in case you didn't know it, toddlers are expensive. They always need things like clothes, food, clean laundry, and, if you're a working parent, day care.

So of course, instead of doing the responsible grown-up thing, like staying in an affordable apartment, or creating and sticking to a budget, I bought a house that came with a mortgage, property taxes, homeowner's insurance, water and sewer bills, and a ton of household repairs for which I was responsible because that's what happens when you're your own landlord.

We spend much of our childhoods yearning to be adults, to get out into the world and make our own decisions. We want to eat what we want to when we want to; we want to buy what we want to when we want to; and we want to be in charge of our own lives. Being an adult and in charge of your own life seems so exciting until you realize it's really a weird mix of daunting decisions and mundane details that need equal attention.

Adulting got very real for me very quickly. Needless to say, I didn't give enough attention to the details. By the time I realized it, I was in over my head. Very responsibly, I made an appointment with a consumer credit counseling agency, where the kind woman there said to me, "The problem is you need to make more money in order to pay all of your bills."

I laughed until I cried. Then I kept crying because I was a teacher, and I wasn't going to be able to make more money unless I took on a second job after school or on weekends…and if I did that I'd have to pay for more child care and wouldn't have more money.

This sad story ends with me declaring bankruptcy by the time I was twenty-seven, getting divorced by the time I was thirty, and starting a whole new chapter in my life.

But *You're* Going to Be a Great Adult

It took me ten years of missteps, but I finally learned how to adult. You're always realizing there's something you or the other adults in your life don't know.

I mean, I just learned that my husband doesn't know how to sew on a button. The man has lived multiple decades as an adult and can't sew on a button!? What has he been doing all these years? Throwing away clothes when the button falls off? Walking around being held together by safety pins? I may have to Google how many allowances to claim on my W-4 form, but at least I know how to sew a button back on my clothes.

The good news is, you get to learn from my mistakes. I'm laying it all out here so you can adult with the best of them. By the time you finish this book, you'll not only know how to sew on a button, but you'll also know answers to some of adulting's most baffling questions: What exactly *do* you say to the doctor's office when you need to make an appointment? And *why* does laundry have to be separated and done so often?

So, keep reading. I promise I'll keep telling you stories of how badly I failed at adulting so it can be easier for you, and you can feel good about yourself! But I'm also going to sneak in the stories of what I've learned to do well over the years, because I need to feel a little bit better about myself, too.

1 | MONEY MATTERS

Budgeting and Balancing

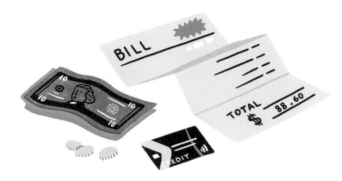

One of the best things about being an adult is that any money you make is yours. If you don't have dependents you're responsible for, you're only accountable to yourself. You can decide how you spend your money and on what. But that's also one of the hardest things about being a moneymaking adult—how to spend it, and on what. The second hardest is that you're accountable for the consequences of how you choose to spend it.

Now, if you're a completely responsible person who never impulse shops or who doesn't ever have the internal debate about whether to buy concert tickets or to pay the electricity bill, you're handling your newfound adulthood better than most of us. Or, you have a great high-paying job and don't have to worry about how to make the most of your money. Either way, I'm envious of you. But most of us need to learn how.

MONEY, MONEY, MONEY

There's a song by ABBA about money that comes to mind every time I'm paying bills. The gist of the lyric is that despite working all the time, once you've paid the bills, there's no money left, which can be very sad. And especially when you're starting out, that can often be true. For a lot of us, our first jobs don't pay very much; so one downside to adulting is that you often must make what feels like tough decisions about spending your money. Having your own money isn't as much fun anymore when you realize how much work you put in to make it, and how little you can use for play. But it doesn't have to be that way. One of the best ways to have more money to play with is to create a budget—and stick to it.

The Hidden Costs of Adulting

Most people will tell you creating a budget is simple—all you need to do is make a list of your monthly expenses, know how much money you have coming in monthly, and then subtract your expenses from your income. And, sure, that's the basics of creating a budget, but there are a lot of factors left out of that equation. There are some questions that really matter.

Why do these questions matter so much? They're what I like to call the hidden costs of adulting. It's easy to remember to add your rent and cellphone bill to your monthly expenses, but when your rent check bounces because you went out for drinks every Friday night, your budget is worth about as much as the paper towel you wrote it on. OK, so let's look at each of these questions carefully to see why they matter. Bear with me here. This is the math I wish I'd learned in college instead of calculus and statistics.

Where to Set Aside Money

Money can be set aside in separate savings or checking accounts (or for long-term savings goals in investment vehicles, such as money market accounts, certificates of deposit, etc., but we won't get into that here). You can have multiple accounts for different purposes (such as larger fixed expenses or unexpected emergency expenses, like a costly car repair). It's often useful to check out what other options your bank offers. You can even set aside money the old-fashioned way—in an envelope, jar, etc.—say, for weekly groceries or for those unexpected times when you need a little extra cash.

Is Your Paycheck Consistently for the Same Amount of Money?

Knowing how much money you make is at the core of your budget. If you work a salaried job, it's easy enough to calculate how much money you have coming in each month. Every paycheck is going to be the same, and you can use that number with confidence. But if you work an hourly-wage job with inconsistent hours, it's not that simple.

Since 2009, the federal minimum wage has been $7.25 per hour, and that's for workers who don't receive tips (those workers can be paid less per hour). Many states have enacted minimum-wage laws that require the rate to be much higher than the federal minimum, but let's assume you don't live in one of those states.

If you're working thirty hours per week at that rate, you'll make $217.50 a week before taxes (as in, that amount is more than what you'll actually see in your paycheck), or about $870 per month. If you're working thirty-five hours per week, you'll make $253.75 a week before taxes, or about $1015 per month. That's a difference of $145 a month in pre-taxed money, which is huge when it comes to budgeting.

So, let's back away from the math, and talk about what that means in terms of actual adulting. What you need to know is the absolute minimum number of hours you'll be working per week. That's the amount of money you need to be budgeting with. If you work more—bonus! You have some extra money to play with.

Do You Get Paid Weekly, Biweekly, Twice a Month, or Monthly?

The timing of bills and getting paid rarely lines up. In my day job, I get paid twice a month—on the fifteenth and on the last day of the month. I used to get paid every other week, which meant that some months I got three paychecks. Of course, that didn't change my yearly salary, but it sure felt like some months I had more money. But I digress.

The point is that my bills aren't neatly split into "bills due on the fifteenth of the month" and "bills due the last day of the month." They're due throughout the entire month. I could just pay them as they come up, and hope that I have enough in my bank account at the time, but that didn't serve me well in the past.

I have to set aside money for each bill from each paycheck. When I worked jobs that paid weekly, I'd set aside a quarter of my monthly rent and car payment each paycheck. Now I get paid twice a month, so I set aside half of those payments each paycheck. The hardest way to do this is if you get paid monthly, bringing us to the next question.

On What Date of the Month Is Each of Your Bills Due?

Some of your bills and expenses will be larger than others, like rent, car payments, student loan payments, etc. My rent always has to be paid by the first of the month, which means I can choose to pay it early using my paycheck on the fifteenth, or pay it just on time, using the last paycheck of the month. Either way, though, it could easily use up so much of my paycheck that there's barely enough left to pay the bills that fall between those two paychecks, let alone to pay for things like groceries. You can work with

Sample Budget for One Paycheck

This is a bare-bones budget that only includes expenses and bills due in the second half of a month, with a paycheck paid twice per month (for example, on the 15th and last day of the month, in this case, on April 15).

April 15-30 Expenses

4/15	Groceries	$75
4/15	Half of rent *(to be set aside for payment in full later)*	$600
4/17	Electric bill	$87
4/19	Phone bill	$50
4/21	Credit card	$45

Total expenses	**$857**
Paycheck *(after taxes)*	$1000
Money left	**$143**

credit-card companies, loan companies, and other providers to change the due dates of your bills, but you're still likely to run into the same issue. Or, you may find that your paycheck arrives just after a bill is due, and you might end up paying late fees. Knowing the due dates of each bill allows you to budget ahead and see how much you need to set aside from each paycheck or from which paycheck you can pay each bill.

Are Your Bills Always for the Same Amount or Do They Fluctuate Month to Month?

It's easy to budget when everything you have to pay comes to the exact same amount each month, but that's not the way it works. Your internet bill, for instance, will usually be for the same amount each month. Your electricity bill, on the other hand, may vary with the time of year. If, for example, you can't stand being hot and sticky and have to turn on the air conditioner or fan as soon as you walk in the door, your bill will jump in hotter months. By the same token, if you live in a colder climate and have electric heat, your electricity bill is likely to be higher during those colder months.

You can budget for variable costs in two ways—always factor in the highest amount you've had to pay, or calculate the average cost over a twelve-month period, and use that number. It works better to go with the highest amount, because it means you don't have to count on having extra during the months when the bill is more.

Do You Have Annual or Semiannual Bills?

These are the costs that catch me off guard. You'd think by now I'd remember my car needs to be registered and inspected annually. Every year, on the same date. It's not rocket science, but for some reason, I'm always taken by surprise. And it's not the only bill like that. If you have an Amazon Prime subscription that you pay for annually, or even a credit card that has an annual fee, make sure you know it. Set a calendar reminder. Write it in big red letters on your daily planner.

Better yet, set money aside monthly for those annual or biannual bills. We do this in our house by having a second checking account (that we didn't get checks or debit cards for). When we get paid, we transfer the money over to the other account to make sure it's not in the account we use for everyday expenses.

It's easier to put aside $18.75 every month than it is to suddenly realize you need to cough up an extra $225 to register your car this month. That's total spitballing on my part. I don't know how much your car registration costs, if you have one. If you don't know either, get in touch with your state's bureau of motor vehicles to find out. Or look at your last registration form, and count on it being that amount. If you're lucky, your car being a year older means it will actually cost you less money.

Is Somebody Else Contributing to the Household Expenses?

Whether it's a live-in partner, roommates, or a relative who helps you pay the bills, having someone else contribute to the household expenses totally changes your budget. It can make it both easier and harder on you. It means you need to figure out how all the bills are going to get paid, and if you're comfortable handling someone else's money to pay them (or having someone else handle yours).

For instance, do you trust that if you give your partner money for half of the internet bill, that money is going to go to the internet provider? Hopefully, the answer is a resounding "yes," but if it's not, then you may want to consider another way to handle paying your half of that bill or investing in your own internet service. (And then put a really strong, encrypted password on the network.)

It also means you have to trust the contribution is stable enough that you don't have to budget for someone else's portion of the bills. If your roommate suddenly gets a job across the country and has to move, can you cover all the rent on your own or find another roommate quickly enough to make sure the rent is paid?

The point is this: Adulting means you have to be prepared to be self-reliant and self-sustaining because life is unpredictable. That may sound like a jaded perspective, but it's also just true.

How Much Are Your Transportation Costs?

Unless you work from home (and even if you do), you're going to have transportation costs. Don't forget to figure out how much you pay for things like gas, public transportation, parking, and tolls, and add it to your budget. Depending on your situation, these may be tax-deductible costs, but they will come out of your pocket first.

Do You Have Prescriptions You Have to Pay For?

My day job provides great health insurance. I pay a decent amount of money in premiums every month, but the coverage is fantastic. But every year, the prescription deductible resets. If you don't know what that means, let me enlighten you (and we'll explore more about health insurance later). My insurance is great, but I have copayments for prescriptions (a copay is what you pay before insurance pays the rest). Once I hit the deductible (the amount I pay each year before the insurance company covers costs), let's assume the copayment is $15 a month for a thirty-day prescription at my pharmacy or $30 for a ninety-day mail-order supply. Or if I take two medications, I have to budget between $20 and $30 a month for prescriptions. Here's where it gets complicated. In January my costs are higher because I haven't hit my deductible yet—the amount I pay out of pocket before those copays kick in. Say that deductible is $1000 a year. Until I've spent that much on prescriptions, it's not $30 a month. It's the difference between what insurance covers for my medications and the actual cost.

If I'm lucky, I don't have a prescription deductible and just have to budget for those copays. (We'll explore this more later.) But if not, I need to be prepared to have a little extra money on hand for January and maybe even February.

Do You Have a Pet?

Pets are awesome. (Unless it's a giant lizard or snake. Then they're a little scary and a good way to make sure you have exactly the right partner or roommate.) Pets are also costly. They need to be fed, for one thing. Let's just start there. Don't forget to feed your pet (that's an adulting fail right there). So, please just add pet food to your budget. And then think through additional expenses like cat litter, pooper-scoopers, terrariums or…whatever it is you need to keep that snake happy, including visits to the veterinarian.

How Much Do You Spend on Groceries Monthly?

Here's the thing about grocery stores: They're filled with food. Food that you may impulsively buy if you go shopping when you're hungry, sad, bored, or tired. And if you don't have a grocery budget set, that organic kale and almond milk you bought because it looked so good may be the purchase that gets you down to your last penny. (OK, yeah it was actually a giant package of Twizzlers, but they looked so GOOD, I just had to have them.) Really, though, if you do nothing else to proactively budget, make sure to decide how much you can afford to spend on groceries each month. Otherwise, all those quick trips to pick up milk and just a few more items are going to add up really quickly.

In our house, we actually grab our allotted food money from the ATM each paycheck and put it in an envelope. Any time we go to the grocery store, that's the only money we spend on food. Anything else we buy, like toilet paper or cleaning supplies, we pay for in a separate transaction using our debit card because it's not coming out of the food budget. Food is paid for with that cash. It's a way to keep track of how much money we're actually spending on food and to hold us accountable for cooking with and eating the food we buy instead of just running out and picking up a frozen pizza because we don't feel like cooking.

When the cash in the envelope is gone, our food money for the month (or that two weeks) has been exhausted. Sure, we had a few rough months at first where we were like, "Honey, what meal do you think we can make with a can of chickpeas, a dried-out lemon, and some ketchup packets?" But we figured out pretty quickly we shouldn't shop without a list and a calculator.

When You Don't Cook, Do You Eat Out or Get Delivery? What About Entertainment?

I wasn't sure if this question should actually be, "Do you cook, or do you eat out or get delivery?" I don't want to assume you cook, but I don't want to assume you don't either. So, let's just get down to it: How much do you spend on restaurant food? Because everyone craves pizza or Chinese food or, I don't know, pie. Put that stuff into your budget. You're going to spend it anyway, so figure out how much you either do spend or can afford to spend monthly, and make sure it's accounted for.

Related is the cost of entertainment. That might be concerts, shows, museums, monster-truck shows, or going to the movies. Assume you do one of these things at least once a month and put it into your budget.

Do You Have Any Special Events Coming Up?

Let's assume the answer to this is yes. There's always a special event because you're newly adulting, popular, and having lots of fun. Or, you know, a lot of your friends are getting married, and you're invited to many, many weddings. You may not have to buy clothes because you have a closetful of event-worthy clothing or good friends to borrow some from. But you might have to buy clothes. That's an expense to keep in mind for your budget.

Other events to keep in mind are things like job interviews, not just because of clothing, but also because of the cost of things like haircuts, manicures, eyebrow waxing, and anything else you may deem necessary to look and feel fabulous. (And I'm not just talking about women here. Men, you too, may be getting your hair and beards trimmed, your eyebrows shaped, and your nails manicured. Don't let anyone tell you that feeling fabulous is gendered.)

Are There Seasonal Expenses You Need to Be Prepared For?

Unless you live on a highly trafficked trick-or-treating route, Halloween candy isn't the kind of seasonal expense I'm talking about. Although—true story—my parents live in the most popular trick-or-treating neighborhood in their town. Everybody drives their kids to this neighborhood, and some years they had over a thousand costumed kids coming to their door. Before the year they decided they were done with it, turned off the lights and went to

3 Automatic Savings Apps to Check Out

 ACORNS is a an app that invests instead of just dropping the money into a savings account. It rounds every purchase up to the nearest dollar and then invests that money, which you can cash out.

 TIP YOURSELF lets you transfer money from a checking account to your "tip jar." You can do it whenever you want. Maybe it's when you skip the $7 latte? Or maybe it's whenever you say a bad word. I'd be broke quickly in the latter scenario.

 CHIME is actually an online bank that offers an automatic savings program. Like Acorns, it rounds up each transaction to the nearest dollar, but instead of investing it, puts that money into a savings account.

the movies instead, they were spending over $100 on candy for one night. Anyway, unless you're moving in next door to my parents, that's unlikely to be a seasonal expense you'll have to worry about. I'm talking more about things like holiday and birthday gifts.

The holidays can be hard on your budget, especially if you're traveling. A friend of mine does something really smart to make sure he has money for the holidays. He uses an automatic savings app. These are apps that round all your transactions to the nearest dollar and then set that extra money aside in an account for you. My friend says he doesn't miss the extra fifty-seven cents at the grocery store and loves having that money available when he needs it. He also says it makes it easier to balance his checkbook because he's always working with even dollar amounts.

CREATING A BUDGET

Congratulations! You made it through the hidden costs of adulting, and you're still reading. That takes fortitude. That list is enough to make anyone say, "Forget it, I'm done being a grown-up. This is just too much for me." But that's the thing about adulting. You can't be done with it. So, let's talk actual budgeting.

Your Monthly Budget Should Balance

Remember I said the woman at the credit-counseling agency told me I needed to make more money to pay all my bills? The hard truth I had to face was that I probably was making enough money to pay my bills. But I made a few big mistakes. Well, if I'm going to be honest, it was one really big mistake that just snowballed. I was too self-assured. Money was coming in, and I didn't know how to track it. That's what a budget does. It helps you track your cash flow. In other words, your budget helps you:

- See how much money you have coming in.
- Know how much money needs to go out.
- Understand how to make it fit together.

A solid budget is the difference between debating if that seven-dollar latte you're craving is worth only having thirteen dollars left to limp through until your next paycheck, or standing in line at the coffee shop knowing that your caffeine fix isn't going to break the bank. It's like the friend who you asked to be your accountability buddy for diet or exercise. (We'll talk more about friends and health later.) Just like you might get annoyed at your friend for reminding you about doing things you may not want to do, you're going to get frustrated that your budget keeps reminding you to think about what you're spending. It's the thinking about it that's important.

A budget is a tool to figure out how to spend your money. It's up to you to decide if you'd rather go to a concert and drink lattes than pay for the basics like electricity or internet. But it's a lot easier to make those decisions when you can see the numbers on paper and really know how much wiggle room you have financially.

1 | Know how much money you have coming in.

It may sound totally basic, but in order to create a budget, you need to know how much money you have coming in every month. As I mentioned before, this may vary if you're working inconsistent hours, but for those of us working salaried jobs, it's a little easier to sort out. Remember to use the net amount on your paycheck, not the gross amount. The net is what you have coming in after all the taxes and other deductions are taken out. British business magnate Richard Branson tells a great story about how he learned the difference between the two from one of his board members. The executive taught him to think about it like fishing. The fish that stay in the net are yours to keep and the ones that get away aren't. So, what stays in your paycheck is your net pay. The other number is your gross pay. Maybe because it's grossly unfair you don't get to keep every penny you make? Moving on.

If you have reliable side gigs or other income streams, add that to the "money coming in" number. Maybe you write books when you're not working your day job. Maybe you sell merchandise with snarky sayings online. The important word is "reliable." If you're not sure you actually have money coming in from the side gig, don't count it. It will feel like a little windfall from the money gods when you do have it. Write down your net income plus your reliable side-gig money. That's the amount you have to spend each month, and it's nonnegotiable.

24

2 | Know how much money needs to go out.

List monthly expenses, making sure to include the hidden costs of adulting. You can do it on paper, make a spreadsheet, or use an app. My husband puts the numbers into a spreadsheet, lets the software do the math, and then creates what-if scenarios that add everything up in different ways depending on which paycheck we pay certain bills out of. I prefer pencil and paper, so I can scratch things out, make notes and mathematical equations on the sides, or crumple up the paper and start again if I need to. To each their own.

Either way, it's helpful to list expenses in order of due dates. So, if you're making a budget for the whole month, and you need to pay rent or your mortgage on the first of the month, it can be either the very last expense of the month or the very first one. I put it as the last one for the month before it's due, so I feel like I'm ahead of the game. It's a little trick I play on myself, so I can pretend I've paid April's rent in March. It's not a particularly effective trick, but to see "March 31: April rent" on my expense list sounds better than putting that large amount of money at the top of my April budget. It makes me feel like I'm starting in a better place.

Make sure you know the date on which all recurring expenses are due in order to know which paycheck they'll come out of. Once you have those listed out, you've got a monthly template to work from. Those dates are unlikely to change, so you can use the same template each month. Once you have all of those expenses listed out, add them up. That's the amount of money you have to spend each month. That number is also non-negotiable.

You also need a way to remind yourself to pay the bills, like a wall calendar with the name of the bill (such as Capital One) written on its due date. Or track due dates in a spreadsheet, duplicating the tab for each month.

3 | Make sure they match up.

Subtract the number from Step 2 (expenses) from your number from Step 1 (income). Ultimately, it's better to have a difference higher than zero, so you can put some money away for emergencies or into a savings account. But sometimes, it's enough to know you can pay all of your bills and spring for some of the extras.

If the difference is zero or above, you have a budget you can live on, and you can skip the next section. I wouldn't recommend it though, because being an adult means you need to have a backup plan in case things like your income or expenses change.

Adulting Tip: Always Start from Zero

If you're doing well with your budget, you probably have money left in your bank account after paying your bills each month, or after each paycheck. But one of the best ways to make sure you don't overspend is to act like that's not true. Pretend you've spent every penny, and start your budget from zero each time. That way, you know that if you have to, you can make it this month if your bank balance is perilously close to going over to the dark side, otherwise known as a negative balance (which will incur bank fees).

When Your Budget Doesn't Balance

This is one moment when adulting sucks, so to make things easier, avoid it if possible. The moment you realize that you have more money going out than coming in is really humbling. It just doesn't seem fair to get to the point in your life when you're free only to feel stuck, frustrated, and maybe even a little scared.

Know the Difference Between "Want" and "Need"

This is when you have to study your budget, take a deep breath, and start cutting your expenses. This is where you separate "want" from "need." You may want all of the streaming services you use, but do you really need all of them? (Hint: The answer is "No." No, you don't need them.)

Do you want to pay your electricity bill? Probably not, but you need to. Think about it: How are you going to watch anything on those streaming services if you don't have electricity? And also, you're going to need lights, hot water, and heat, which, in many places, relies on having electricity.

It's painful, but if your budget doesn't balance, you're going to have to cut down to your "needs" before you start adding in "wants." It's possible you'll also be able to still have some of the things you want by cutting down other expenses.

Maybe you've allotted more money than you really need for groceries, and you can reallocate some of that money to something else. Maybe you can cut down on eating out, and instead host a potluck with your friends, and watch a movie on the streaming service you can now afford.

Which Bills Can You Pay a Bit Late?

Ideally, if you juggle your wants and needs, you won't have to pay bills late. You'll pay everything on time, have a perfect credit score, and will be a budgeting superstar. But even stars get into tough situations. Cars break down, or you have to restock a refrigerator because a three-day power outage made the food you bought the day before the power outage unsafe to eat. Stuff happens, and the bills still have to be paid. If that were to happen to you, know what your bill hierarchy looks like. It's a lot like Maslow's hierarchy of needs, which says physiological needs come first. Maslow, who was a psychologist whose work was focused on happiness, defined physiological needs as the biological requirements needed for a person to function optimally. Those are things like air, warmth, sleep, food, shelter, and clothing. The hierarchy is a pyramid, so those are at the base, and thus must be satisfied before other needs above them.

Air and sleep are free, so you don't have to put them on your bill hierarchy. But shelter, warmth, and food are imperative, which means rent should be at the bottom (most important), as should basic utilities and money for food. After that, you're going to want to pay bills that will charge a late fee, report your lack of payment to credit agencies, or sic a collection agency on you. To be clear, the latter two usually only happen after you're at least thirty to ninety days late on a payment. But late fees are bad news. I've really never

Maslow's Hierarchy of Needs

Maslow's hierarchy is comprised of five tiers depicted as levels of a pyramid, with needs lower down (the base of the pyramid) that must be satisfied before needs higher up. From the bottom upwards, they are physiological needs, safety needs, love and belonging needs, esteem needs, and self-actualization (achieving one's full potential).

SELF-ACTUALIZATION

ESTEEM NEEDS

LOVE AND BELONGING NEEDS

SAFETY NEEDS

PHYSIOLOGICAL NEEDS

understood why you get charged more money when you don't have the money to pay in the first place, but it happens. And it can add up quickly.

Next are things that make it easier to make money. If you need to drive to get to your job, make sure to pay your auto insurance. If you work from home and rely on Wi-Fi to do it, pay your internet bill. Everything else is higher up on the pyramid, so pay those bills as soon as you can.

Reach Out and Ask for Some Lenience

Hopefully, you'll never be in the position of not knowing how you're going to pay all of your bills, but it's an unfortunate reality for many adults. People get sick. They get fired or laid off. Companies go under. Pandemics shut down the economy for months at a time. If something bad happens and your ability to pay your bills is uncertain, let companies know. It may feel embarrassing, and you may worry that they're not going to care, but calling companies to let them know that you're in a bad place financially may actually bring you some temporary relief from payments. You'd be surprised how often the people on the other end of the phone know exactly what you're going through and want to help.

Some loans, like car loans, will let you skip a payment, and add it to the end of the loan instead. Student loans can be put on income-based repayment plans or in temporary forbearance (payments are postponed or reduced, while interest continues to accrue). Credit card companies may waive late fees. Utility companies are often willing to work out payment plans, and so are places like hospitals.

Being proactive makes a difference. Companies are much more willing to work with you if you call before your bill is way overdue. By then, they know you're having trouble paying the bill. But they don't know that you feel awful about it. That's what they need to know—you know you can't make the payment, but you really do want to come up with a solution.

Do You Really Need to Balance Your Checking Account?

You have your budget. You know the money coming in has to match or exceed the money going out. So how do you keep track of how much money you have at any given time? I used to think it was as simple as logging in or using my bank app to look at my balance. The money in the account is what I have to spend, right? Wrong. That's how much money is in the account now, but it doesn't reflect automatic payments or checks that haven't cleared yet.

When my daughter got her first checking account, I tried to teach her how to balance it. If I remember, she said, "Mom, nobody writes checks anymore!" She's not totally wrong, but automatic payments and debit cards work the same way. It's money coming out of your checking account you have to be aware of and account for.

Before we used apps like Venmo or Zelle to pay for things from a linked account or card, people carried a checkbook where they recorded the checks they wrote. At the end of the month, you'd check your account statement against your checkbook register to make sure they matched up. Many of us no longer carry around checks and record expenses by hand in a checkbook register, but we still use a traditional checking account as our primary bank account. Our paychecks are typically direct deposited into it, our debit cards are linked to it, and we pay our bills online from it. And there may be times when you actually need to write a check. While many people do not have a physical check register to balance, you still need to reconcile your records with your bank statement. Here are some examples why.

It Helps You Avoid Costly Mistakes

If I give my child-care provider a check for $175 the night before balancing the account, and the balance shows $225 the next day, it doesn't mean I have that much money to spend. If my child-care provider didn't have time to cash or deposit the check, that $175 hasn't come out of my account. I really only have $50 available. If, instead of balancing my checking account, I spend $60 more, not only will the check bounce, but I'll be $10 overdrawn with a bounced check fee on top of it. That's one reason to keep your checking account balanced.

Fraudsters Are out There

Last year, our debit card was cloned. My husband balances the checkbook almost daily, and noticed some weird charges. Somehow, we were spending money in Minnesota, Kansas, and California all on the same day. We live in Maine. We were both in our living room. It wasn't us. We called the bank and reported the suspicious charges, so they could reverse and investigate them. Then we called the police, who asked if we'd been to the local gas station recently. It turns out someone had put credit card skimmers on the gas pumps.

Banks and Merchants Make Mistakes

While companies are basically honest, errors are sometimes made, whether by humans or machines, that may result in charges to your account that you didn't make. You want to catch those errors as soon as possible and bring them to the attention of the bank or merchant.

Balancing Your Account Isn't Hard

Keeping a close eye on the transactions in your checking account is key to proper money management, and balancing your account isn't hard. Whether you decide to use an app, computer software, or an old-fashioned manual check register, just do it.

1 | Record your transactions.

You can do it with an app, personal finance software, a basic Excel spreadsheet, or an old-fashioned check register. You should always keep track of the date, amount and to whom a transaction was paid (or deposited), including any ATM transactions and checks written.

An old-fashioned (but simple) way to record things that covers all you need to keep track of is included on what's called a check register. If you got checks when you opened your checking account, you may already have one. It's the booklet side of the checkbook—the other side is blank checks. A check register has columns and rows to note transactions, the date on which they're made, and to add or subtract those transactions from your balance. See the example on the next page.

However you do it, keep a list of every transaction you make, including any checks you write, debit card transactions, deposits you get or make, and money you pull out at the ATM (along with any fees that come with that). Some people might tell you to do this as soon as you make a transaction (whether using an app on your phone, writing it in a check register, etc.) but that's not always practical. You can definitely do that as you're paying bills at home in your pajamas—that's the joy of the internet. You can enter each amount into your register after you enter a payment into the computer, knowing the amount you gave to your credit card company correlates to actual money coming out of your bank account.

The Old-Fashioned Checkbook Register

You can record transactions in many ways. Whether or not you write checks, an old-fashioned check register is a simple way to show how it's done.

- **Check number:** Ignore this if you don't use checks.

- **Date of the transaction:** This is important to note so you can match it against what your bank statement shows.

- **Transaction:** This is where you write the name of the person or business you paid, either by check or by debit card. You may also want to note the confirmation number of the payment or the account number if you're paying a bill.

- **Debits, payments, bank fees or withdrawals:** If you're noting money that you've paid out, this is where you put the amount.

- **Checkbox:** Check when matching transactions to bank statements.

- **Deposits, Credit:** Note money coming in.

- **Balance:** Add or subtract after each transaction, and write the new balance here.

You'll have to enter other transactions after the fact. That's why it's good to keep your receipts when you buy something, or take money out at an ATM. I recommend setting aside time at the end of each day to enter these into your app or check register. Otherwise, you may find yourself behind in balancing your account, rifling through all of your clothes to find the crumpled receipts you shoved into a pocket to get out of the way of the person behind you at the bodega who was inching up to pay for his sandwich before you were done at the register. As long as you do the math, you should have a good and accurate sense of your balance.

2 | Reconcile against your bank statements.

If your records are up to date, you might be able to wait until you get a monthly bank statement to reconcile it to your account. This statement can be found in your account online. Starting at the top of the statement, find the transaction in your records, and mark it as correct (if you're using a checkbook register, for example, check it off in the checkmark column). Then you can see if there's anything on your bank statement that you forgot to record. If you're lucky, it was a deposit you didn't record or know about. If you're not, it was a couple trips to the ATM you forgot to record. You can add that transaction to correct the balance in your records.

My husband reconciles our account every couple days, and it's a good thing, too, because there are always little things that don't make it into the records, like that episode of *90 Day Fiancé* I rented on a whim when I climbed into bed. And if you're an insomniac who binge-watches shows, those little charges add up quickly.

3 | Don't disregard transactions not cleared.

Sometimes the bank says you have more money than your records say you do. In the best of circumstances, it's because you made some foolish little math error, but usually, it's because you've subtracted all of the bills you've paid, and some of them haven't cleared the bank yet. From the bank statement's balance, subtract payments in your records that have not yet cleared, and add deposits that have not yet cleared. This is the amount you have once all transactions have cleared.

4 | Deal with any weirdness.

If your balance doesn't match and you can't find any errors or transactions not accounted for, you may need to go back further, or ask someone at the bank for help. If you find charges you know you didn't make, let the bank know ASAP. You want to get on it as soon as possible so any other suspicious charges will be flagged. Depending on your bank and how soon you report the fraudulent charges, you may be on the hook for some of the money or have to wait until they finish the investigation to get the money returned to your account. Let the bank representative know if that's going to be an undue hardship. When the gas station bandit cloned our debit card, our bank account balance was perilously low. Once we explained to the bank what was going on and they had confirmed that we'd filed a police report, a very sympathetic bank manager overrode the waiting period and returned most of the money to our account, so we could pay our bills.

ABOUT CASH AND CREDIT CARDS

Before we move on, I have a few thoughts regarding credit cards and cash. It can be easy to think credit cards are the way to patch the holes in your budget. Because the purchases you put on credit cards don't have to be accounted for in your checking account, it may feel like you're not truly spending money. But you are. It's just money you don't currently have.

Have a Credit Card Available for Emergencies

You need a darn good definition of emergency, because when you're just starting out as an adult, credit cards can be a path to destruction. My friend Jess told me she got a credit card in college just to get the Jimmy John's sandwich that came with it. She was hungry, she said, and she wasn't going to use the card anyway. Flash forward to now. Jess still has that credit card, with a fairly substantial balance on it. She says that sandwich was totally not worth the debt.

To Use or Not to Use Your Credit Card

Use your credit card sparingly (or not at all, if you can't control yourself), and save it only for emergencies. I cannot stress this enough. Don't charge stuff to your credit card if you can't pay off the balance within a few months. If you can do that, it's a great way to build good credit (which gives you the ability to borrow money later when you really need it, such as getting a car loan, for example). But if you can't, it's a great way to get sucked into a black hole of debt. If you can only make the minimum payment each month, you're barely covering the interest charges on most cards. No amount of airline miles or a Jimmy John's sandwich is worth watching that debt grow. What good are airline miles if you can't afford the vacation once you get somewhere?

Always Have Some Cash on Hand

I learned from the debit-card-cloning incident to always have some cash on hand. And by on hand, I don't mean in my wallet where I'm tempted to spend it. I mean like in an envelope in a safe place in my home. I started pulling out about $20 or so every time I got paid and setting it aside. That way, I won't be caught in a situation where I have no money at all if someone clones my card again, or the power grid goes down and stores can't take cards. I call it my apocalypse money.

Don't Expect to Be Perfect

Hopefully, you'll be smarter than I was when I was younger, and stick to not spending more money than you make. But here's the thing: You're going to make mistakes. You're going to accumulate overdraft fees. You're going to pay a bill late once in a while, either because you just forgot about it or because you spent the money on something else.

You'll probably find yourself digging through your pockets and couch cushions for cash or returning bottles at the end of the month to make it through to your next paycheck (if you live near a facility that lets you recycle for cash). For some people, it only takes a couple of overdraft fees before they reevaluate their budget. For you, it may take a couple of calls from a collection agency to realize you have to make some changes. Mistakes help you figure out what you're comfortable living with, and what you're not.

2 |
GETTING AND KEEPING A JOB

Work and Career

Getting a job is a critical step for successful adulting. It's how you have the money to do all the things adults do and to pay all the bills adults have to pay. Keeping a job is equally important. After all, paying bills and having nice things relies on a steady influx of cash, not just sporadic checks here and there. That is, unless the work you do is seasonal or pays unusually well for a short period of time. I suppose if you're a roadie touring with a band, you may make good money while the band's on tour, and may not need to work when they're not. But most of us need to get and keep a steady job.

TACKLING THE JOB HUNT

Job hunting can be a challenge, but you will find one eventually, even if it's a job with a lowercase "j" that's a stepping-stone to the Job with a capital "J" that starts your career. How do you make that happen? It starts with knowing not only what you want to do, but also how you want to do it.

Freelance or Full-Time?

This question is misleading, because freelancing, for the most part, is a full-time job, one that millions do instead of working for an employer. I started out working for an employer, then as a freelance writer and consultant. Now I work for an employer and freelance on the side.

The Benefits and Downsides of Freelancing

Being your own boss has its appeal. You make your own hours, you don't have to worry about being micromanaged, and you get to make the mistakes we all make in the early years of our career while you're only accountable to yourself (in principle—though you are accountable to your clients). And depending on what you do for work, you can work with more than one company at a time. For example, if you're a "creative," (think, to name a few: graphic designer, writer, web developer or programmer, costume designer, or public relations professional), it gives you a chance to build relationships with different companies, publications, clients, and organizations before settling down. And if you're not sure you're ready to be around lots of other people in an office, it can be a good way to dip your toes into working with people without having to do it every single day.

Freelancing also has drawbacks. For example, you must buy your own health insurance. (*Don't* think, "I'm young and healthy, I don't need health insurance." Accidents and unexpected illnesses happen.) You must pay self-employment taxes, which, if you don't set aside enough during the year or pay quarterly, can be a very large sum of money the IRS expects on Tax Day. And freelancing can be more than full-time, because there's the work and the hustle. Unless you have long-term contracts with clients, you're always pitching new ones, trying to renew contracts, or realizing you're three months away from no work at all. You must convince people you're best for the job, your idea is worth taking a chance on, and follow up on getting paid. Because not all clients pay on time. (Or at all. But that's another problem.) If you love being around people, freelancing may not be for you. Unless you have to be onsite for a job, you'll likely spend lots of time working by yourself, with your own thoughts, wondering if you spoke to another human today.

The Benefits and Downsides of Working for an Employer

If freelancing doesn't sound right for you, your other option is to find an employer. There are many benefits that come with that, not the least of which can be a steady paycheck, as well as benefits, like health insurance and tax withholding (so you can get care when you're sick and not have to pay gobs of money to the IRS on Tax Day). Other benefits can include paid time off and sick days. You don't have to spend time chasing work, and may have chances for advancement.

There are many types of employers: small businesses, large companies, nonprofits, and so on. Today's job market also allows for movement without anyone thinking much of it. These days, people tend to move between companies and occupations more fluidly than they used to. You don't want your job history to show that you change jobs every six months, but it's not unusual to move on after a couple of years.

If you like being around people, there will be people to interact with, and get to know, because they're the same people you'll be working with daily. Being sociable with your coworkers can lead to great friendships that can last a lifetime. I would also be remiss in not mentioning that some employers and offices also have snacks and coffee. That is a huge draw.

As for the drawbacks, there's a difference between the downsides of working for your specific employer and working for an employer in general. Only you know the details of why you may or may not want to work where you work, but a lot of specific complaints tend to be around company culture, not liking the people you work with, feeling undervalued, having a tyrannical boss, or being overworked.

The downsides can be more of a bummer than a deal-breaker. For instance, having set work hours, reporting to someone overseeing your work, or not being able to choose your work assignments can feel confining. For some people, working for an employer can mean navigating more complicated things that can feel chafing, things like strict rules around social media conduct or even intellectual property rights. (In fact, if you're an inventor, professor, or someone who creates for a living, it's likely that the rights to anything you invent, publish, or create during your period of employment belong to your company. Make sure you read the fine print before you sign a contract, if you're offered one (though most jobs don't actually come with an initial contract; you are typically given an employee handbook after you're hired).

Redefining "In Your Field"

When you're looking for your first career-building job, it can be easy to get stuck on not finding job openings in "your field." Let go of the idea that the perfect job will have a title that completely matches the one that goes with your degree. Think outside the box a little! Search for jobs by required skills. You might be surprised by how quickly your definition of what's in your field opens up.

My sister has a degree in library science, and after working as a reference librarian, she's now a communications specialist for a nonprofit that publishes scientific journals and books. I also have a friend who has a Bachelor of Arts degree with a concentration in acting. He works as a professional fundraiser. He's vivacious, great with people, and knows how to be "on" when it matters.

Rules of Networking for Newbies

Honestly, the old adage, "It's not what you know, but who you know" isn't totally untrue when it comes to getting a job. And that means you're going to have to network. Go to conferences and industry meet-ups. Take a friend who works for the company you want to work for out for coffee. Follow-up by responding to the email your mother's cousin's friend's neighbor sent you. If you're a networking newbie, here are some basics.

1 | Do your research.

Before heading out for coffee, happy hour, a conference, or whatever professional event you're going to, know what you're walking into. Check out the LinkedIn or company profiles of people you'll meet. (That way you know what they look like, if you've never met them in person.) Look over the attendees and speaker list for conferences, figure out who you want to talk to, and do some research on them, too. When you meet them, it gives you a chance to have a conversation about things that are important to them. Just be careful—if your research methods include a deep dive into their Instagram or other social media feeds, don't lead with questions about their pets or last vacation. That shows you've done a little too much research.

2 | Get your elevator pitch down.

I thought "elevator pitch" was an old-fashioned term, but that changed when I went to a conference where people had to wait three to five minutes for the elevator. I'd never been so happy to have my thirty-second sound bite about myself, what I do, and why I was at the conference. An elevator pitch is a quick synopsis of

How to Create an Elevator Pitch

Even though your elevator pitch is spoken, it's a good idea to write it out ahead of time so you can practice. Focus on what you do, what's unique about what you do (or about you), and what you want to do.

You're trying to impart what distinguishes you from everyone else and what your goals are. For example:

"I recently graduated with a degree in social media marketing, and had the chance to intern with some amazing people and brands while still in school. I'm looking for a job where I can use my skills to create compelling, memorable campaigns for social impact."

your background that's short enough to present during an elevator ride. The goal of your elevator pitch is to have a concise, engaging overview—who you are, what you do, and what you want to do—that makes people want to know more. If they're backing away from you or their eyes glaze over, you need to hone your pitch.

3 | Use the phrase "Tell me about yourself."

Networking is about building relationships. People like to talk about themselves and to know that other people are interested in them. After I introduce myself to people and give my elevator pitch, the next thing I tend to say is, "Tell me about yourself."

Try to use the person's name if you have it. But not in a creepy way or too familiarly. If you're talking to an expert in your field and they're referred to as "Dr. Expert," don't take it upon yourself to use their first name when you first meet them. The people you meet appreciate the chance to tell you about what they do and what their company does. It's also a good chance to find—and please hear my eyes rolling when I use this business buzzword—synergy between what you do or want to do and what they do.

4 | Use professional language, even in casual settings.

I love the F-word as much as the next person, and I tend to use it more than the average person. I've read that swearing is a sign of intelligence and who the f*ck am I to disagree with that? It's not in my professional vocabulary, though. You may swear with your friends, and in general, society has loosened up a little around it, but it's still not acceptable in a professional setting. You never know who isn't cool with a few F-bombs or other choice words.

Try to tone down filler words, such as "like" and "umm," too. They detract from your message. Another tip I learned from an expert communications trainer is to avoid starting sentences with "I think" unless you're asked what you think. Otherwise, drop the phrase. You're the expert. You don't think. You know.

5 | Ask for and offer a business card.

You're going to meet 1,001 people at networking events. About 800 will be like you, looking to connect with people who are more ahead in their career than you. The rest of them, you're going to want to remember and know how to get in touch with. Practice the phrase, "It was great talking to you. Do you have a card?" You'll probably get it. Then follow up with, "Thanks! Here's mine." You can also give someone a card if they don't have one for you. (And if you're in the midst of a pandemic, or it's more convenient, you can take photos of cards with your phone.)

Have Business Cards on Hand

Business cards are pretty cheap to create and order online. (You can even print them at home with the right supplies and templates, if you're good at that sort of thing). They don't have to be fancy. Keep it simple: name, phone number, professional social media profiles, and professional email address (it's time to dump beerchugchamp@wherever.com and get a new one). And don't describe yourself as a "generalist" or use some vague title on your card. If you don't have a title, just leave it off and offer to write a little note on the back of the card indicating what you discussed and who you are.

6 | Make notes for yourself.

Likewise, make notes to yourself on other people's business cards. Not necessarily in front of them as that can be awkward, but afterwards. It's hard to remember who's who from a card, especially if you're in a situation where you're meeting a lot of people, and you'll want to remember what you talked about. It's how you start a conversation via email or phone when you follow up after the event. If you write on the back of the card, "Talked about how the price of oil is impacting the industry," that's your opener for a follow-up email.

7 | Follow up in a few days.

If you take the card, found the conversation helpful, and said you were going to follow up, do it. Don't wait weeks to follow up. Send a quick email in the next few days reminding them you met, what you talked about, and something that shows the conversation was meaningful. It could be as simple as:

"It was great to meet you at the conference. I'm sure you might still be digging out from your email, but I started some research inspired by our conversation about oil prices. I came across this interesting analysis and wanted to pass the link on to you. Can we schedule some time to discuss this more?"

8 | Keep the connection open.

Even if people you meet don't lead to jobs or mentoring relationships, keep the connection open. If they work for a company or in an industry you'd like to get into, ask about company culture, whether they anticipate hiring anytime soon, and if there are any challenges you might help solve. (Yes, it sounds intimidating, but the worst that can happen is that they say no.) And don't forget your new contacts have contacts of their own. If you check in every few months or so, it will keep you on the radar. Just don't check in too often or on a set schedule—that can come across as too eager and single-minded.

Applications, Résumés, and Cover Letters, Oh My!

It would be nice if all you had to do to get a job was network, meet the right person, and get hired on the spot. But that's rarely how it goes. You're going to have to fill out job applications, write résumés and cover letters, and put yourself out there. It takes work to get work. But once you do it a few times, you've got the basics handled, and then it's just about tweaking here and there for the specific position.

Filling Out Job Applications

Most applications are online, which is both good and bad. It's good when you upload your résumé to a job-seeking site or LinkedIn (which you absolutely should have a profile on) and just hit the "Apply Now" button. The application autofills your info. All you have to do is double-check it and add anything that's missing. But it's bad when you're filling it out on the employer's website and the connection times out so you lose all of the information you've already put in.

It's a good idea to cut and paste what you've written into a Word document every so often, or write it out in the Word doc first, and then cut and paste. I suggest the latter as it gives you the chance to do a grammar- and spell-check before sending. But don't be afraid to reach out and admit if you mess up an application. True story: I landed the gig that launched my career because I accidentally sent a typo-riddled version of my résumé for a job, and realized it after I hit send. After a few minutes of agonizing, I looked up the hiring director's email, wrote an email saying I'd inadvertently sent the wrong version of my résumé, and would she please read the new one attached? My willingness to reach out, admit my error, and correct it made me stand out as an applicant. Not that I'd recommend anything like that on purpose—just know mistakes can be handled. Here are some mistakes to try not to make in the first place.

Applying to a Job You're Over- or Underqualified For

This is a chance to let your confidence shine. Note that you know you're overqualified, but really thrilled to have the chance to learn from so-and-so at the company. Or if you appear underqualified, make sure to say you have life experience that makes you perfect for the job even if your degree may not indicate it.

- **Not following directions.** Some applications or job listings have things buried in the instructions to see if you're paying attention. And some people don't read the directions. Don't be that guy.

- **Not filling in all the fields.** Better to write n/a (not applicable) than leave a field blank.

- **Making spelling or grammar errors.** Don't forget to proofread. If you're not entirely confident in your own proofreading skills, ask a friend to take a look before you send off your application.

- **Leaving gaps without explanation.** There's nothing wrong with time in-between jobs or after graduation, but if it's more than six months, it may be worth noting the reason in your cover letter. For example, if you traveled, say so, and add a bit about what you learned while doing so.

How to Write a Résumé

Writing a résumé begins with staring at the blank page for half an hour, sighing, Googling résumé examples, coming back to the blank page to stare some more, and then wandering off for a snack. After that, it's time to get down to it.

So, here's what a résumé is not. It's not a list of every job you've ever had. It's not an inventory of every skill you possess or every award you've gotten since middle school. And it's not a magical document that's going to get you the job. It's a fancy flyer that's going to convince hiring managers you are worth talking to. Here's how you get past staring at the blank page.

1 | Pick a format.

- **Reverse chronological order** is the most typical way to format a résumé. It has some flexibility and shows off your experience. It's good to show career progression, especially if you're applying to a job in a field similar to the one you're working in now, and want to show you've moved up the career ladder.

- **Skills-based** is better if you're just out of school or changing careers. It focuses more on skills than experience, and then you don't have to include the job in retail or food service that you worked at to put yourself through college or, you know, to pay the rent.

- **Combination** is just what it sounds like. It combines the other two résumé formats to show off your experience and skills. It's great if you're a career chameleon that has a lot of different skill sets or wants to work in more than one industry. It doesn't need to be tweaked as much for each job.

JAYSON JONES

(555) 555-5555 | jj@wherever.com | LinkedIn URL | Facebook URL
YourPortfolioOrBlog.com| Twitter Handle | Instagram URL

KEY SKILLS AND TOOLS

- SEO-based content strategy
- Social media channels and platforms: Facebook, Twitter, Instagram, Tumblr, YouTube, Pinterest, Hootsuite, WordPress, Bit.ly, Google Analytics, Libsyn, Sprinklr
- Software: Adobe Photoshop, Adobe Illustrator, MS Office Suite
- Reporting tools: PRWeb, HARO

OBJECTIVE

Young professional with a passion for storytelling and a desire to work for a large public relations agency. Graduated Cum Laude from [your college] with a bachelor's degree in digital marketing and social media. While in college, I interned at [agency] and [agency] where I had the joy of planning, implementing, and executing social media campaigns. Worked closely with clients to assess their needs, desired outcome, and ideal customer base in order to proactively design social assets and content calendar.

EDUCATION

B.S., Digital Marketing and Social Media
Your college, Sometown, State
Certifications: Hootsuite | Google Analytics | Microsoft Teams & Tools

EXPERIENCE

Social Media Management Intern
Different Agency, Sometown, State / 2019-2020
- Managed social media strategy for Client X
- Served as point of contact for influencers on Campaign X
- Monitored online presence for Campaign X and engaged proactively with users to strengthen customer loyalty

Social Media Management Intern
Agency, Sometown, State / 2018-2019
- Designed social assets
- Identified and managed relevant influencers
- Created and managed social media calendar

2 | Get your info in order.

I assume you know your name, mailing address, phone number, email address (the work-appropriate one), and your website's URL (if you have one). You're also going to need to know where you've worked and approximately from when to when for each job, and a brief description of your responsibilities for each role.

3 | Write a résumé intro or objective along with skills.

Your intro is a few sentences or a short paragraph at the top of your résumé or LinkedIn profile summarizing what you can do. It's geared toward catching an employer's eye. You might hear this called your career objective or qualifications summary. You can inject a little personality, but don't come across as flippant. Then list the key skills you have (see sample résumé). Here's an example for LinkedIn (similar to the résumé example, but including skills up top):

Young professional with a passion for storytelling and a desire to work for a large public relations agency. Graduated cum laude from [your college] with a bachelor's degree in digital marketing and social media. While still in college, I took the opportunity to intern at Edelman Digital and 360i where I had the joy of working on campaigns for social impact organizations.

Background and skills include: SEO-based content strategy | Hootsuite-certified | Google Analytics | Microsoft Teams & Tools

4 | Showcase relevant work experience.

The key is to choose what's important. It's the core of your résumé, so you want it to shine. You listed your skills, now prove you know how to use them. Phrase what you did at previous jobs using some of the phrases the job application you're looking at includes. You may have created spreadsheets and twiddled your thumbs at your last job, but you can rephrase as, "kept organized, detailed database of customer information," and "spent time ideating on innovative solutions."

5 | Build an education section.

If you're a college graduate, that's where your education section starts. If not, make sure to include the name of the high school you graduated from. Include:

- The degree(s) you received
- Universities, colleges or technical schools you attended
- Their location in city, state format
- Any other certifications or courses you've completed

There's debate as to whether you should include the year you graduated as well. It's up to you, but it can clue people into the fact that you're just beginning your adult life.

NAILING THE JOB INTERVIEW

You've networked, crafted the perfect résumé, filled out a gazillion-and-one applications, and now you have the job interview. Hooray! Now is when the game really begins. Your fate is in the hands of someone who doesn't know you except on paper. They're going to talk to you for maybe an hour and decide if you're the person they will pay money to do the things that need getting done.

Take a breath. You're going to be OK. You already know you're talented and delightful. Now's the chance to show that in a way your job application and résumé can't.

Business vs. Business Casual vs. Casual

Business

Masculine:
- Button-down shirt with light pattern and tie
- Blazer or suit jacket
- Dress pants in brown, navy, or black
- Clean loafers or lace-up dress shoes

Feminine:
- Monochromatic or subtly patterned blouse
- Blazer
- Knee-length skirt or dress slacks in neutral tone
- Closed-toe dress shoes

Business Casual

Masculine:
- Collared shirt or sweater with light patterns
- Khakis, corduroy, or colored denim pants
- Casual dress shoes

Feminine:
- Subtly patterned or colored tops
- Mid-thigh to knee-length skirt or dress with tights, or dress slacks
- Dress shoes (open- or closed-toe)

Casual

Masculine:
- Nice T-shirt or collared shirt
- Presentable jeans
- Sneakers

Feminine:
- Nice T-shirt, collared shirt, or fitted blouse
- Presentable jeans or pants
- Sneakers or sandals

Dress for Success (Really)

It's not always clear what each company's dress code is. Even if they say, "business casual," what's the difference between regular casual and business casual? Or the difference between business and business casual? Although I did once have somebody tell me that "cocktail attire" is just business casual with lipstick on. I hope this is helpful advice to you. It wasn't to me because I still hadn't figured out business casual.

My rule of thumb when it comes to job interviews is that it's better to be too dressed up than underdressed. You can always remove a suit jacket or blazer or a tie or necklace once you get in the door if you feel overdressed compared to the people in the office, but that doesn't work in reverse. If you know somebody who works there, ask him or her what you should wear to your interview. Or, you can scope out pictures of the office on job-seeking sites if they're on there. If you're really worried about it, you could also stroll past the office the day before your interview and watch the people going in and out of the building. But that's a little over the top. Instead, go with some basics:

- **Err on the conservative side.** You don't want to be like my friend, who wore a great, new, beautiful silk blouse to a client meeting without doing the "lean over" check. That's the whole thing you do where you bend over a little to see what shows or how clothing shifts. Hers shifted drastically. As in, full-on wardrobe malfunction.

- **Don't wear anything too new.** I'm not suggesting you show up in worn-out clothing. You just don't want to be wearing shoes that pinch or pants that bunch up uncomfortably for the first time at a job interview. If you buy new clothes, do a test run at home first.

- **Avoid perfume or cologne.** You never know who might have allergies. You don't want to be remembered as the reason the interviewer had to step out for an antihistamine or an EpiPen.
- **Lose the logos.** Don't wear things that have messages or logos printed on them. Not until you get the job and they ask you to wear their logo.
- **Keep jewelry to a minimum.** This isn't a "cover your tattoos and remove your nose ring" suggestion. That's yours to decide. It's a suggestion to wear just enough jewelry to look and feel put together and not so much that it distracts the interviewer in person or clinks and jingles during a video interview.

What Not to Say at a Job Interview

Some interviews are very situation oriented and ask you, "What would you do in X situation?" Those are tough, but they're a good opportunity to show your problem-solving skills and talk about times you've faced similar challenges. Good interviewers embrace silence before jumping into the next question to see what you'll do with it. Don't say any of the following.

1 | "So, what is this job?"

Remember to do your research and read the description before you apply for the job. Come in prepared. If you want specifics on the job responsibilities, you can ask about that later.

2 | "My current company is a hot mess."

It may be true, but the interviewer is going to wonder what you'll tell people about their company if you end up working there.

3 | "It's on my résumé."

Whatever "it" is, the interviewer wants to know about it now. Answer the question and expand on the skill or experience they're asking about.

4 | "I only have X amount of time for this."

Block off at least thirty minutes more than you think you'll need. If by some chance, the interviewer is really late, politely ask if you can make a call to let whomever you need to know you're going to be late, or ask if you can reschedule.

5 | "I'm an outside-the-box thinker. Would you like me to unpack that?"

Insert any business buzzwords. Don't use them unless you know what they mean and have something to say that demonstrates it.

6 | "I don't know."

There's nothing wrong with not knowing an answer to a question. What's wrong with this is that it doesn't show any motivation to find out or give the interviewer anywhere to go. Instead use a bridge phrase to talk about something related to the question that you do know. "I don't know about that, but what I do know is..."

7 | "This is a great entry-level job for me."

Don't give the impression you're planning an exit before you even get in the door.

Questions to Ask in a Job Interview

At the end of an interview, you'll likely going to hear, "Do you have any questions?" Make sure you have some. It shows you've put thought into it and are interested. Here are some to have ready.

1 | "Can you describe the day-to-day responsibilities of this position?"

You want to know what you'll be doing each day. It also gives you a chance to see if what they tell you matches up with what you thought you'd be doing.

2 | "How would you describe the company culture?"

The answer to this question may not be as telling as someone's body language or choice of words. And if you're being interviewed by more than one person and they exchange a "you go first" glance before answering, you may want to dig a little deeper.

3 | "What's your favorite thing about working here?"

This is a good follow-up to the company culture question. You're listening for true enthusiasm and a little bit of thought. A canned, cheery answer would make me a little nervous.

4 | "Do you anticipate this role evolving over time?"

Many companies or start-ups have an all-hands-on-deck way of working. Knowing whether this role fills a specific need and will continue to can help you know if you're entering a culture of uncertainty. That may be what you're looking for, but not everyone is.

5 | "What are the next steps toward an offer?"

This says, "Hey, I'm interested," but it also says, "Hey, I think you're interested, too." Asking it this way cuts to the chase. You don't want to know what happens for them to make a decision. You want to know what happens in order for them to make an offer—to you. Those are two different things.

Now That You've Got the Job Offer

Congrats on getting the job! You worked hard for it. So hard in fact, that you probably need a vacation to recover from job hunting. Now's the time to find out if you can take one. Not a pay-money-go-somewhere-exotic vacation necessarily, but more like a "phew, I have a week before I start the job" vacation. When you get the offer, you don't have to jump on it right away, either.

You can ask when they need your answer by, which gives you some time to make sure it's what you want and to call any other job leads that haven't come through with the offer yet. Sometimes it can spur them to make a decision if they know you have another offer. But not always. Just know that.

Navigating Salary Negotiations

It's important before accepting a job offer to know how much money you're going to make. Many people don't ask because it's uncomfortable, or because it feels unseemly or as if we're being grabby. But the truth is, that's the reason most people work. To make money. You didn't go through this whole process because you wanted to volunteer forty hours a week.

Ask the question. "What's the salary range for this position?" Asking about the salary range shows you know most places have some wiggle room when it comes to salary. If the answer is, "The salary for this job is X," and that's it, you have no wiggle room. If there is a range, however, be bold and be brave. Know what the lowest you're willing to work for is, and ask for more than that.

The internet is awesome (we've established that) but in this case, it's awesome because it will tell you what the typical range is for this type of position. Ask for something in the middle range, the kind of money someone who has a few years more experience than you might be getting.

Wait until you get a clear answer before letting them know you'd work for less. If they don't meet your offer, but offer a salary at or above what you're willing to work for, it can't hurt to ask if you might be able to get additional vacation time instead. Just don't be arrogant or desperate. Don't take less than you're worth, but don't overestimate your worth for a first career path job either.

Accepting the Offer

Know what's expected at that salary. If you're going to be working a sixty-hour week for $40,000 a year, is that worth it? Maybe. Who am I to say? I jumped for joy at an $18,000-a-year teaching job. Also, get it in writing. Know what the parameters of your job are, the benefits that come with it, and the salary you're being offered, so everyone is starting on the same page. A page, I might add, that you can then refer back to if things go a little sideways when you start the job.

Once you say yes, it's time to get details. When do you start? Who do you report to? Is there an orientation and training schedule? Do you need to do paperwork first? If there is a contract, read it before you sign it, and ask any questions that might come up. Many jobs, however, do not have contracts—at the very least, be sure you have a clear job description. Stand your ground if there's something you're not comfortable with, and suggest a change if necessary. If there is a contract, get a countersigned copy once you've signed it.

Filling out Paperwork

Being an adult involves paperwork. And starting a job means so much paperwork, much of which confuses the hell out of me. Here's a quick rundown of the things you need to know.

What Numbers Do I Need to Know?

Employment paperwork asks for numbers. Not just your phone number, but emergency contacts, social security number, maybe your driver's license number. If you don't have these memorized, have them with you. Bring your social security card or passport, because most U.S. employers need a copy of government-issued documents to prove citizenship. (We'll cover more about identity later.)

What's the Difference Between a W-4 and a W-9?

A W-4 is the form you fill out to tell your employer how much money to withhold from your paycheck to cover taxes. The more you have withheld, the more likely you are to get a refund in the spring, but your paycheck will be smaller. There's information on the IRS website that can help determine withholding, as well as other online resources to help you potentially achieve a balance between getting enough in your paycheck and also paying enough taxes so you don't owe in the spring. A W-9 is the form you fill out if you're not an employee but freelancing or contracting. You share your tax information so the company or client can report to the IRS how much they paid you. It's how the IRS knows how much self-employment taxes you owe come spring.

Avoiding Potential Office Pitfalls

Working for an employer usually means being around the same people day in and day out. It can be hard being the new person in a workplace, especially when everyone else already knows each other and how things work. Interloper or new office hero, here are some ways to avoid getting in people's metaphorical way at your new job.

Learn the Office Culture

There's a difference between company values and company culture. Values are what the company believes in, and employees need to live up to those values in the workplace. Culture is how people interact with each other. Some companies are all business and encourage keeping it that way. Employees work together during the day, some are friends, but most of them go home and hang out with friends who they don't work with.

Other companies have a culture in which employees on the same level work together and hang out together. Still others encourage everyone to work together and hang out together. Regardless of which culture your company strives for, there are always going to be people who don't adhere to that culture and that's OK, too.

Get a Copy of the Organization Chart

To that end, know who works with and for whom. Ask for a copy of the organizational chart so you know who's in which department and who's in charge of supervising which people and projects. If there isn't an org chart, ask someone in human resources if they can verbally walk you through that information. (Larger companies have a human-resources department, while smaller companies may only have one person who handles human resources.)

Ask Questions

You're not going to know how to do everything at your new job. Don't struggle through trying to figure it out. Ask someone to show you, take notes, and then the problem is likely to be solved. (See also: Choose a Mentor Wisely, below.)

Choose a Mentor Wisely

Find someone who's been there longer than you. Ask them to show you the ropes or if they're willing to answer questions. It should be someone you feel comfortable with and whom you've seen other people interacting with in a way that shows mutual respect.

Confidential Means Confidential

Assume that anything you learn about the company, its strategy, and its clients is confidential. And if you signed a non-disclosure agreement (NDA), assume you might be taken to court if you share that information with anyone. I know more than one person who has gotten fired over accidentally sharing company secrets after a few too many margaritas.

But Confidences Aren't Always Confidential

Don't trust the person who asks you all about your personal life on your very first day and then tells you they know everything about everybody, "so if you want to know the scoop on someone, just come find me." That tends to end badly. That person won't keep any of your secrets because your secrets are social capital to them.

Moving up the Ladder

Hopefully, you've found the perfect job at the perfect company and you want to move up the ladder. Moving up takes more than just doing your job well and having good performance evaluations. It means looking out for new opportunities inside the company, too.

Know Your Worth

This is advice I'm not so great at myself. I always underestimate my value and only realize it when someone says to me, "You do know that everyone thinks the world of you and your name comes up for every project, right?" You'd think after hearing that a few times, I'd be like, "Of course I do!" But, no, I'm always surprised.

Don't be me. Pay attention to how people respond to you, how often they come to you for advice, thought leadership, and more. Write it down if you have to. Then use that as a negotiating tool when you want a promotion or a raise.

Asking for a Raise

The best advice I ever got about asking for a raise was from my friend, Jen. Jen said, "What would a man do?" Men, I'm sorry, but that's damn good advice to give a woman. A lot of men don't hesitate to ask for the raise. That's not to say they're not anxious or nervous about doing it. But maybe less apologetic.

Say, "I'd like to talk to you about the work I've been doing," and then outline all the work you've done, how it's benefited the company, how much profit or attention it's brought in, and then get right to the point: "It's time to renegotiate my salary."

That's the way to do it. Show you know what you're worth, and back it up with numbers and measurements. Don't talk about how your rent increased or that your long hours mean you're paying the dog walker more money. That's not the point. The point is you're doing exceptional work, and you'd like that to be reflected in your compensation.

So, if you know all of that to be true, you know the company isn't going under financially or laying people off, and that you're not at the top of your salary range, do it. Ask for the raise.

3 |
LISTEN UP

When to Talk,
When to Stop, and
How to Say It All

Part of being an adult is being able to communicate with people in many situations. The laws that let you make your own decisions once you're a legal adult also mean you must speak for yourself. Even if you want your mom to call the doctor for you, she can't always do that because of privacy laws. You can ask your mom to tell you what to say, but she can't be with you everywhere you go and in every conversation you have. That means it's up to you to communicate with people—and not just people you know.

Frankly, it's not always easy. I still ask my husband to call in takeout orders if I can't do it online. I don't like talking to people on the phone. What if they judge me? But it doesn't really matter what the stranger on the other end of the phone thinks of you unless you need their help with something and you're being a jerk. What matters is that you know how to talk to them. So, let's dive into all the ways adults have to communicate with each other.

Making Small Talk

Being an adult often means finding yourself in groups of people, some of whom you don't know, at a party, a work event, or some other meet-up. That means making small talk. That's a weird phrase, "small talk". It's so backwards because conversation with people you don't know should be called "big talk". It's a big deal to talk to people you don't know and may not like, and it can feel like a big waste of time.

Disregard advice to talk about the weather. It isn't interesting, and once you've established that it's been warm lately, you're back to staring at your wine glass and feeling uncomfortable. But the people you're trying to talk with may be just as uncomfortable as you. They'd rather be having a meaningful conversation, too. How many times can you actually talk about the weather in one evening? So, be interesting. Talk about things that matter and make you happy.

It's not always easy to manage conversation in social settings. And there's always at least one person who loves being the center of attention, dominates conversation, and has Stories with a capital "S." That may be you. If it is, thank you. You're the person I try to hang around with at events so I don't have to talk as much. But if that person isn't around, here's some advice on how to start navigating conversations.

Jumping into a Conversation

Group dynamics can be tricky. Each one has a different personality and a unique communication style. Jumping into a conversation means paying attention to body language. Are you approaching a private or open group? If people are looking around and seem open to you, you're probably in the clear. You're also going to want to pay attention to the rhythm of the conversation before asking, "Do you mind if I join you?" If the pause in talking is a natural lull, go for it. If someone is just taking time to breathe, wait for that natural lull.

Don't be the one who jumps in with something unrelated to the conversation. There's a balance between sounding like you've been eavesdropping and are barging in. Phrases like, "I couldn't help but overhear," work better than, "You know what might help that rash you were talking about?" Use your good old-fashioned "wh" questions—who, what, when, where, and why—if you're trying to get up to speed.

That's going to sound different depending on the conversation you're entering and how well you know the participants. Here are some examples:

- If you know the people in the group really well, you might ask: "OK, who has the awful rash and is it contagious?" or "When did it first appear?" or even "Why aren't you headed to the ER?"
- If you sort of know the people in the group, you might ask: "Sorry if I missed this; what show are you talking about?" or "Why do you think they killed off his character?"
- If you only know some of the people in the group, you might say, "Sarah! It's so good to see you again. Where do you all know each other from?" or "What are you talking about and do you mind if I join you?"

Starting the Conversation

Starting a conversation involves a bunch of things you have to evaluate in the moment, such as knowing if it's the right time to have a conversation. You have to be able to recognize nonverbal cues that the other person wants to talk. It's easier to see when they don't. They'll avoid eye contact, start walking away, turn away from you a little as you approach, and other things like that. It's a good idea to start with a basic greeting instead of just jumping in mid-thought.

Don't assume because you recognize somebody that they recognize you. It's embarrassing to say, "Jake! It's so good to see you again," and then realize you've never actually met and, in fact, you just follow him on Instagram. You may want to be a little more low-key. "Hey, I don't know if you remember me. I'm Amanda, and we met…" or "Hi, I'm Amanda. I recognize you from Instagram. You post some really thoughtful / weird / funny stuff."

Keeping the Conversation Going

What's harder than starting a conversation? Continuing it. It takes work, especially if you regret starting it in the first place. The fact is, it can be hard not to get stuck in your own head and think about what you want to say next. But when you do that, you don't pay attention to what the other person has said, and they can sense that. Try to ask follow-up questions to indicate you've heard what they've said.

If you can't think of anything to add or ask, keep an arsenal of words or phrases you can use to show you're paying attention, like "Right" or "Yeah?" Just mix it up a little because saying the same thing over and over definitely sounds like you're not really paying attention.

Ending the Conversation

It's time to end the conversation. And if you feel creeped out or uncomfortable, it's totally fine to say, "I've got to go," or "Excuse me," and walk away.

Some people aren't skilled at reading nonverbal cues of someone trying to end a conversation, like checking the time or turning away. That's when you want to start using verbal cues and saying things like "So..." or "Well...." If the person still doesn't get the cue, be clearer. Use a closing sentence like, "It was good talking to you," or "Well, I have to get going now." And then...get going!

Learning How to Listen

A big part of communicating effectively isn't about talking; it's about listening. Active listening is a technique that comes in handy, especially during tense conversations and conflict.

1 | Be attentive.

Active listening means giving the person you're talking with a safe space to speak. Pay attention not just with your ears, but with your body, too. Lean in a little, focus on the other person, and don't think of how you will respond. You need to hear what they're saying.

2 | Be open.

Have an open mind. You might not agree with what they're saying, but be open to hearing a different perspective, and respect that the person may have views on the situation that differ from your own. Try not to criticize, argue, or try to change somebody's mind when you're listening to what they're saying. To be clear, though, this doesn't apply to things like racist or abusive rants. You don't have to consider the perspective of someone who is actively offending you or a group of people.

3 | Ask questions.

If you don't understand what someone's telling you, ask questions. Try to stick with open-ended questions that can't be answered in one word or phrase. It lets the other person say what's on their mind without feeling like you've already sized up the situation.

4 | Summarize what you've heard.

Summarize key themes, but don't assume you've understood. State in your own words what you think they've said, giving others a chance to correct misunderstandings. "Let me summarize to make sure I'm understanding... Is that accurate?" Summarizing helps make sure both of you feel like you had the same conversation, heard the same things, and have come to an understanding.

Speaking Up the Right Way

You may be good at active listening, but not everyone is. Being an adult means you have to speak up when you feel misunderstood, misheard, or misconstrued. Those things happen a lot.

If you're in the middle of a big meeting, it's not the right time to say to your boss, "You never listen to me! I suggested that three weeks ago." But if your boss is misinterpreting your words or taking credit for your work, there's nothing wrong with saying something like, "Just to clarify, when I made that suggestion, what I meant was [insert your smart idea here]."

Speaking up in personal relationships can also be tricky. As I've gotten better at adulting, I've also gotten better at thinking through what's important to take on, what's not, and the most productive way of speaking up. That's not to say I always do it well, just that I think about it more now.

In the past, I may have lost my temper over a butter knife left at the edge of, but not in, the sink, even though I made it clear it's a pet peeve. I may have put the knife in the sink as loudly as I could, sighed, and stomped around. But you know what? There are bigger things to worry about than misplaced butter knives. I'd rather put the knife in the sink, let it go, and take on bigger things that might actually make or break a relationship. You decide what that is for you. Just remember two things:

- You're more likely to be heard if you think through what to say beforehand and calm down before starting the conversation.
- Even if you have a good point, people rarely hear what you're saying if the way you're saying it is off-putting. Try to keep your volume and tone of voice in check.

THE ART OF APOLOGY

Sometimes you'll say or do things you shouldn't have. Giving a genuine apology is part of adulting. As kids, we're taught to say, "I'm sorry," when we hurt someone's feelings. But it doesn't mean anything if there's nothing else with it. It's a way of telling someone, "I said the words, now get over it." Saying, "I'm sorry," without context isn't the only way to not apologize. You've definitely seen or heard a non-apology. It's why the phrase, "Sorry, not sorry" is a thing. Just look at some of the statements celebrities put out when they do or say something insensitive or awful. They may say, "I apologize if you were offended," or "I apologize for saying X, but what I meant was…" The first puts the responsibility on the person offended, not the person who did the offending. The second says there was a good explanation for why you did something rotten.

Steps to Making a Genuine Apology: SORRY

So how do you apologize and actually mean it? Just keep the word SORRY in mind. Each letter is a step in building a genuine apology.

S = Stand up

Recognize what happened and how it made the other person feel. Acknowledge you did harm, no "buts" about it. "I'm sorry I called you that name."

O = Own it

Once you acknowledge you caused harm, own your actions. It's not just that another person was offended. You're responsible for that offense. "I was angry and I overreacted."

R = Respond differently

Think through how you wish you'd handled it instead, and say it out loud. "I should have taken a moment to collect myself before I spoke."

R = Repair the damage

Sometimes it's easy to fix the damage. If you break something, you replace it. If you fail to do something and it's not too late, do it. Other times, there's no fixing it, so you may need to ask what you can do to make the situation better. "What can I do to help you move past this?"

Y = Yield to the other person's feelings

You can't make someone forgive you. You can say the right things, but that doesn't erase the hurt. "I know you're still upset and not ready to forgive me."

Staying in Communication

Communication is a two-way street. When you're out on your own for the first time, it's easy to forget that not everybody in your life knows each other. It's also hard to remember that sometimes you're going to have to be the one to reach out to others.

Create an Emergency Contact List

In our smartphone society, many people don't have landlines or numbers memorized. Update the medical ID or In Case of Emergency (ICE) contacts in your phone. You never think you'll need them until something happens.

Like getting heatstroke when you're on a work trip, causing you to barf in front of your colleagues, and then pass out while sitting at a high-top table in a restaurant with your ankles wrapped around the stool's rungs because you're too short to touch the floor. When you hit the ground, passed out, you also break your ankle. And because you're unconscious, having your ICE set on your phone is the only way someone knows how to get in touch with your emergency contact. That's a true story. The punch line now is, "It was the first time the EMTs had ever picked up a sober person from the floor of a bar!" The punch line then was, "Oh, crap!"

Put the names of the people you want contacted in an emergency, with their phone numbers and relationship to you in your phone. You can even just put it there as a saved memo. Make sure you have a written copy or a document saved to the cloud, too, in case you need to reach people and your phone is stolen, missing, or dead. You may even want to keep a piece of paper with the info in your wallet or purse.

Getting in Touch

Lots of communication is done without talking to someone. I love that I can text my hairstylist to set up an appointment, she can text me to confirm, and I pay her through Venmo. I don't really have to talk to her at all if I don't want to, although I do when she's cutting my hair. But not all communication should be done without talking to someone. Let's look at when it's OK to call vs. text vs. email.

When Do I Need to Call?

- Emergencies: Including apartment maintenance emergencies, like a broken pipe or a thermostat that won't turn on in winter.
- Older relatives: Check with them, but if your relative signs a text message, "Love, Aunt Barbara," it's probably a good chance you should be calling her instead of texting or emailing.
- Time-sensitive issues: Like getting prescriptions filled, making sure your employer knows you won't be coming in that day, or making a doctor's appointment when you're really sick.
- A return phone call is required if somebody asks you to call back. (But you're off the hook when it comes to telemarketers who leave random messages.)

What to Say When You Call

Phone calls can be unnerving, especially if it's somebody you don't know. Just keep it simple. Here are a few basic phone scripts:

- "Hi, my name is Lauren. I live at 55 Hope Lane in apartment 2C. I'm calling about a plumbing issue. I'm at 555-5555. Thanks."
- "Hi, I'm [NAME]. I'm calling for [NAME]. Are they available?"
- "Hi, [NAME], this is [NAME], I'm calling to follow-up on [THING YOU BOTH KNOW ABOUT]."
- "Hi, I'm calling to see if you have [THING YOU NEED] in

stock? You do? Great. Can you put it aside for me?"

- "Hi, this is [NAME]. I'm a patient of Dr. Expert's. I'd like to make an appointment, please."

When Is It OK to Text?

Text anybody who would text you instead of calling. In fact, I prefer you text me to tell me you'll call me, so I have time to prepare. You can text anybody who says they're easier to reach by text, whether it's your landlord, boss, or hairstylist. If they said so, it's OK to do it.

And it's OK to text to check with someone you'd normally call if you don't have the time, energy, or privacy for a phone call. Let them know it's a quick check-in so they don't freak out that you're avoiding them.

When Is It OK to Email?

Emailing a business to ask a question you don't need a fast answer to makes sense if they have their email address on their website. You can email your doctor's office for non-time-sensitive questions, too.

And it's fine to email friends, but not to e-blast all of them about something, put all their email addresses on cc, and open everybody up to the dreaded Reply All. If you have something you want to email blast, like a party invitation, at least put people on bcc.

Any correspondence you want to keep a record of that doesn't need a formal letter should be emailed, including emails to your employer, landlord, ex, and the airline you're trying to get a refund from. If you wouldn't want anybody to see what you've written in an email, a good rule of thumb is to not send an email. You never know who forgets to delete the previous thread before forwarding an email, who will forward an email without thinking about it, or who would forward an email if you made them mad enough.

Dos and Don'ts

You probably won't need to make small talk, speak up, apologize, make phone calls, email, and text all in one day. But keep these basics in mind.

DO: Be Clear

Say what you need, why you're talking to someone, and what you are hoping to gain from the communication. Use specific words as opposed to vague ones like "thing," "stuff," and "it." Expressing yourself clearly cuts down on people misreading you. Re-read emails and texts to make sure your meanings are clear.

DON'T: Be Passive-Aggressive

Passive-aggressive is when you say and act as if you're OK with something, but you're not. It's passive-aggressive to expect others to know what you need or want and then be angry when they don't meet an unvoiced expectation. Don't expect people to know what you mean if you say the opposite. Most people take what others say at face value. If you say, "It's fine, I don't mind doing the dishes," don't expect them to guess if you're really not fine, or understand why you're angry at them later for something they didn't know bothered you.

DO: Say What You Mean

Say what's on your mind (as long as it's appropriate). This is the opposite of being passive-aggressive. Instead of expecting people to read your mind and follow your unspoken expectations, tell them what you need and want. You can also tell them what you don't need and don't want.

DO: Let Things Go

Other adults will do things that bother you, or make you mad. Deal with those feelings and fix what needs fixing in the relationship, and then let it go if you can. You don't have to forget; you just have to stop dwelling. If you can't, it may be time to rethink the relationship.

DON'T: Be Unresponsive

If somebody tries to communicate with you, don't ignore them (unless you have a restraining order, or have told them outright to stop contacting you). If you can't talk, send a text saying you'll get back to them. If you need space, say so. If you don't have the mental bandwidth to consider their request, ask them to call or email you back in a few weeks. Showing that you're willing and able is a big adulting win.

4 | SHOULD I POST THIS?

Navigating Social Media

You've used social media since you were old enough to open your first MyFaceTwit account. It can be a great way to connect with people; to share experiences, ideas, jokes, and memes; and even to keep track of the great meals people make and eat. It's also a great way to see trolls in action and be insulted by strangers.

Social media sometimes brings out the worst in people because they assume they're fairly anonymous. But, as all of us have seen play out, assuming you're anonymous on social media doesn't mean people can't figure out who you are. With adulting comes a responsibility to think through the rewards and consequences of how you use social media.

Social Media = Social Responsibility

One of the things I like best about social media is staying in touch with friends near and far. I may use it to rant, rave, or complain about things. Usually, I do that through private messaging, but once in a while I've posted something before thinking it through or made a comment that came across differently than I intended.

There's nothing wrong with saying what you mean, but people read things through their own lenses. If they disagree, they may think you're trying to start a fight when you're sharing a differing view, which can lead to ad hominem attacks. (That's when someone comes at you personally and insults you as a way to undermine your argument. It can get nasty. Believe me. I've had it happen to me, and it can get ugly.)

Having conversations about things we disagree about is fine, but it's also important to do it in a way that can't be held against you. Think about the features on your favorite social media platform. Is there an edit function? Is there a way to delete comments? That's good because you can go back and clarify or delete what you've posted. But it also means other people can edit their comments in a way that makes your reply sound unreasonable or harmful, or delete the comment you're replying to. What you post can be held against you—by family, friends, schools, employers, and, in extreme cases, law enforcement.

How Do You Want to Be Perceived on Social Media?

Many people use social media not only as a way to express

thoughts, share pictures, and connect, but also to create a persona. If people don't know you in real life, the persona you put forth is easily mistaken for the person you really are. That doesn't mean you have to expose everything about yourself, but it does mean that you may want to err on the side of not looking too perfect (this is not a problem I have) or too unpleasant.

Sarcasm and a couple F-bombs may show you're human. However, consistent bad language, crude jokes, or provocative photos show more than that. It creates a persona that your friends—online or in real life—may enjoy and want to hang out with, but one that might not make a good impression on other people. The person behind that persona is more likely to be turned down for jobs, and miss out on opportunities to meet people you'd really hit it off with. Think about how you want to come across to others on social media, decide on your guardrails, and before you post, ask yourself if what you're about to send out into the world is how you want to be perceived. Social media can be unforgiving, so think before you post.

Will You Want to See This Ten Years from Now?

One of the tests I use when posting is to ask myself, "If I got super-famous and some envious wannabe dug this up ten years from now, would it hurt my reputation?" It's served me well. The "Do I want to see this in ten years?" rule is also good when it comes to posting photos. I mean, there's always the scenario in which a future partner may not want to see you draped all over an ex, but there are also the ones in which you look back and think, "What was I wearing? What was up with my hair? Who is that person I'm with, and why are they holding my head while I puke in the street?"

Will You Want Your Mother to See This Ten Minutes from Now?

That's extreme, but there are smaller examples. Do you want your mother to know that you hooked up and had the best sex of your life last night? What you don't mind seeing ten years from now may be something you don't want your mother to see ten minutes from now. Keep that in mind, too. You can adjust privacy settings on some social media, but not all of them. And don't underestimate other people's willingness to start drama by taking and sharing screenshots. If you don't want your mother all up in your business, don't over share. In fact, don't over  share if you don't want anybody all up in your business. If you just can't resist posting stuff like that, at least consider creating an account under a pseudonym or nickname.

A Cautionary Tale

A friend of mine documented the breakdown of their marriage in real-time on Facebook, from the moment they discovered their spouse cheating to tagging that spouse in posts and saying all the things you'd say to someone after catching them cheating, but publicly. It unfolded for days in front of all their Facebook friends, with people weighing in on one side or the other. It was really uncomfortable to see, and even after my friend calmed down and took down those posts, the damage had been done. Not only were friends taking sides, someone apparently took screenshots that were then used in a custody battle once divorce papers were filed.

Social media isn't a place to air your dirty laundry. Think of it this way—if that story had ended differently, and my friend got back together with their spouse, all of that information was out there. How would other people who felt strongly that one of them was righter than the other be able to resume an easy friendship with them as a couple? How would they be able to have a nice Thanksgiving dinner with family after that?

Social Media and Your Career

Your social media behavior will impact your career. It just will, and maybe not in the ways you'd expect. You probably already know that a raunchy social media presence or badmouthing your current or former employer may affect your ability to get a job. You may not know that potential employers use social media to do research on you. It's the first thing I do when I need to hire somebody or am offered a contract by a new client. I jump on my computer and start searching.

A 2018 CareerBuilder survey found that 70% of employers search social media sites to research candidates. And while a little over half of them found something that made them decide not to hire someone, 43% found something that made them want to hire the candidate.

That's good news. If your social media presence comes across as professional, backs up that you have the skills for the job you applied for, and shows that other people interact positively with you, it may land you a job. The flip side is that not having an online presence at all can hurt your chances in some cases. That same survey found that one in five employers expect a job candidate to have a digital footprint. So don't forget to create a LinkedIn profile or update the one you already have.

Cleaning up Your Digital Footprint Before Job Interviews

Things will pop up on the internet about you that you can't control. I cringe every time I see some of my older headshots pop up, but because they're attached to articles I wrote years ago, I can't take them down. They belong to the client for which I wrote them. I can, however, control posts people can see if they're researching me. You can, too.

When you opened your first social media account, you were probably thirteen years old. Do you want the things that thirteen-year-old posted to be what a potential employer sees? Please, let the answer be "No!"

Lock down privacy settings that allow you to restrict who sees your content before you start job hunting, so posts aren't visible to the public. Un-tag yourself in photos that may be offensive to anyone who might hire you. Lean on the side of conservative when you think about what might be offensive or sway an opinion. That means not just photos of nights out on the town, but also things like attending protests, smoking, drinking, and maybe even bathing-suit photos. Scour your accounts to find any unflattering posts you may have made about previous jobs or co-workers. Then, delete them.

What's Your Company's Social Media Policy?

Not only do companies sometimes monitor employee social media accounts, they also tend to have policies around acceptable use. If you aren't given a copy of the social media policy, ask for it, and then read it thoroughly. And then ask for clarification on things you don't understand.

If you use social media as part of your job, there are likely to be rules around what you can and can't post. If part of your job is to maintain a company social media account, don't use that account for personal things. Create a separate personal account and clearly indicate in the "About" or "Bio" section which account is which. Make sure people clearly see that your personal opinions are yours and not held by your employer. My personal Twitter bio for example, says "Tweets=mine." Keep in mind, too, that if you're an employee at will (which most of us are—it means we can be dismissed by an employer for any reason), and something you post goes viral in a negative way, it can get you fired. It happens all the time.

Should You "Friend" Your Boss or Co-workers?

Many workplaces encourage a culture of everybody being friends. That's fine in person, and going out for drinks or doing team-building activities together may be something you have to do. That doesn't have to extend to your social media accounts. If you are truly friends with your co-workers or boss and you trust them to see the messiness of your personal life, go ahead and connect with them. But know that what you say may come back into the workplace to haunt you. If you just want to vent about your crappy day at work, and you're friends with your co-workers, they're going to see that. A lot of people I know don't friend anyone they work with until they or the other person moves onto another job.

THINK BEFORE YOU USE SOCIAL MEDIA

Hearing a theme? It really boils down to THINK before you post.

Is it   **T**rue?

Is it   **H**elpful?

Is it   **I**nspiring?

Is it   **N**ecessary?

Is it   **K**ind?

What a Repost Says about You

You don't just have to think about what your own social posts say about you. You also have to keep in mind that what you repost or re-tweet reflects on you, too. It's not just the content. Sometimes the content is awesome, but the profile is sketchy.

Don't just evaluate whether what you're passing on is accurate (use Snopes.com liberally) or helpful, but also take a look at the source. If the rest of their content isn't anything you'd get behind or there's something in their bio that makes you uneasy, don't repost it. I tend to not repost anything from any account that doesn't have a full bio or a real avatar. That "RT ≠ endorsement" line in my Twitter bio may make me feel better, but when it really comes down to it, I can't count on people to look at my bio to see that. A couple of tips:

- Read the full article, not just the headline or social media recap. Same with videos—watch them all the way through before sharing them.
- Think through whether you'd have created that post yourself

if you'd had the chance. If there's hesitation, you probably shouldn't share it.

- Try to see other perspectives before sharing. If content might disrespect or hurt someone whose opinion matters to you, don't take the risk.

The Rules of (Social Media) Engagement

1 | Take your emotional temperature.

You've probably posted things you regret. I have. It's hard to take something back once it's out there. You can apologize, but people can't un-see what you posted, even if you delete it. Take a moment or gut check with a friend before going off.

2 | Deal with private issues privately.

If something one of your friends says offends you or you need to tell them what you think and don't want everyone else to see, do it via private message. Or, see rule 1 to be sure it really matters before sending the message.

3 | Ask before tagging people.

My friends know I want photo approval before they tag me. Most of the time, I want to approve the photo to be sure I look good in it. Nobody likes to be tagged in a picture that makes him or her look bad in any way. So ask permission or comment in some way that says, "Let me know if you want me to tag you!" That's especially true for group photos.

4 | Know it may get negative.

I don't know how many times I've written a post or started to share an article and then went, "Nah, I don't want to deal with the backlash." If you know your post may be controversial or just annoying, be prepared to deal with the negative responses. Deal with them calmly, that is.

5 | Know you may only be funny to you.

Humor doesn't always come across the same online as in person. Your family and friends may know when you're being ironic, but a broader audience might not. I tend to use a lot of (KIDDING) in my posts.

6 | Protect privacy.

You don't want to put yourself in situations where your reputation, be it personal or professional, will suffer. You also don't want to put yourself in jeopardy of being doxxed (having private information posted about you) or hunted down in person. But make sure you're doing the same for other people you might tag or mention in anything you post. Don't share private information on public channels.

Nothing Is Really Private

You've locked down your privacy settings; deleted all the things you wouldn't want an employer, your mother, or your significant other to see; and taken all the photos off your phone and put them onto a flash drive. You're good, right? Wrong. This may sound like total paranoia, but privacy on the internet is a construct. Nothing is really private.

As long as there are options to share, the ability to take screen-shots, cloud-based storage, and the Wayback Machine (a digital archive of the web), you're better off with the mindset that your posts, likes, comments, content, pages, and photos can be located and traced back to you. For good measure, also assume you'll make someone mad enough at some point that they'll want to get back at you. That's probably never going to happen, because you're super-likable, but maybe someone won't like you because you're so darn likable. People are unpredictable.

Google Yourself Regularly

If I had to sum up navigating social media as an adult in three words, those three words would be, "Set Google Alerts." Not for the sake of vanity, though it's cool to have things roll into your inbox because you did something newsworthy. Nope, set Google Alerts for your name and Google yourself regularly to make sure your reputation is staying clear.

You never know when someone might grab one of your posts and embed it in another post in a way that makes you look bad. To be clear, they can also make you look good. You also may never know who else in the world has the same name as you and is up to shady sh*t. You want to stay on top of that in case your employer also has a Google Alert set for your name and doesn't read carefully enough to be sure it's not you, or if there's a manhunt and someone pulled your picture instead of that of your name-twin.

Living in a digital world means digital upkeep, but I know you've got this. Or, you're going to stay off social media entirely. Either way, you're going to be fine.

5 |
YOUR IDENTITY

Driving, Voting, Residency, and More

You've learned a lot about life skills—finances, getting a job, communication. These are fundamental. But adulting isn't all about personal responsibility. It's also about being an engaged citizen and taking advantage of the rights and privileges that come with that.

Getting Your State ID, Driver's License, or REAL ID

You probably already have a state photo ID or a driver's license, but if not… To get a state ID without driving privileges, just visit your state's bureau of motor vehicles, and follow the guidelines for application, which usually include providing documentation of your legal name, date of birth, Social Security number, residence, and proof of citizenship. Like getting a driver's license, you will have your picture taken and pay a small fee.

Getting Your Standard Driver's License

Maybe you don't have a driver's license yet. Of course, you first need to learn how to drive by getting a learner's permit (which usually requires passing a written or online test) and practicing driving, either by taking classes or with a courageous friend or family member. This should also include finding out what your state's road test looks like, so you can practice that specifically. When you're ready, get on your state's department or bureau of motor vehicles website and request an appointment for your road test, which you will need to pass in order to get your license. Make sure that you also know what other documentation you may need to bring with you to apply for your license. And once you are a driver, remember that almost all states require drivers to have a minimum of active car insurance to drive legally.

I grew up in a rural state and was able to get my driver's license at fifteen, but despite taking driver's education and doing all my required practice hours, I failed my first road test. It was parallel parking that did me in. I turned the wheel too soon and hit the car I was parking behind. I learned that when you hit a car during your road test, the test examiner drives you back to the DMV. Needless to say, I can now parallel park perfectly because I practiced obsessively before my next test. What's the moral of the story? Practice as much as you can before your test.

Getting the REAL ID

You may already have a driver's license, but if you want to travel by air, even if it's domestically within the United States, without a passport, you'll need to upgrade. As of October 1, 2021, in order to get on a plane without a passport, you'll need to have a REAL ID—a license or ID that has some additional requirements. If you're travelling  by air internationally, you'll still need a passport, but to travel by air within the U.S. or to get into federal facilities, like federal courthouses or military bases, you'll need a REAL ID with a black or gold star at the top.

To get your REAL ID, you're going to have to go to an office of your state's department or bureau of motor vehicles, and wait until it's your turn. Grab a book, download a movie or some awesome podcasts, and just do it. But call first. In many states, you need to schedule an actual appointment to get a REAL ID. And you'll need to bring a bunch of paperwork with you. You need to:

- Have something that proves you're a legal citizen of the U.S.

or living in the U.S. legally, like a passport, birth certificate, or naturalization certificate.

- Be able to show your full legal name, date of birth, and your Social Security number.
- Have at least two documents that prove your home address, such as insurance cards, rent receipts, or utility bills.

Other Times When You Need to Get a New Driver's License

Sometimes, you'll just need to replace an old driver's license. Here are situations when you may need to do that:

- **You move to a new state.** Most of the time you can transfer the license from your previous state and not have to take any of the tests again (but not always).
- **You lose your driver's license.** Unless you're my friend, who has the most amazing meet-cute story that happened because he left his license at a bar one night, and then got it back and met his awesome boyfriend, you're going to need a new one. A replacement license can usually be requested online and tends to have a minimal replacement fee.
- **You've recently immigrated to the U.S.** Until you establish residency, you can use an International Driving Permit (which allows you to drive in another country as long as you have a domestic license in your home state or country) alongside your non-U.S. license. Once you've established residency, you'll need to get a state driver's license.
- **You're coming close to your current driver's license expiring.** In most states, your driver's license is current from two to ten years. Thank goodness if your state sends you a reminder close to when it's going to expire (not all do), because ten years is a

long time. You'll probably have to go to the bureau of motor vehicles in person to get a new picture taken. I mean, think of how different (or more put together) you might look ten years after your first license picture!

- **You've had your license suspended or revoked.** No judgment. You'll have to prove you've done what you needed to after the violation. You may also have to provide documentation from your auto insurance company showing the minimum required liability insurance. In some states, you might have to pass the road test again, too.

Steps to Becoming a Voter

Having the freedom to enact change as a voter is pretty cool. What's even cooler is that in some states, you can vote in primary elections (to select party candidates for upcoming general elections) if you're seventeen, as long as you'll be eighteen by the time of the general election. Almost every state requires you to register to vote, which usually requires an address from which you plan to vote, as well as some form of identification, such as a driver's license or Social Security number. There may also be a registration deadline before Election Day. And in over half of the states in the U.S., you need to show identification, often a valid photo ID, to access that privilege on Election Day, especially if you're a first-time voter. The right to cast a vote to make your voice count isn't the only right you have. You have other rights as a voter, too.

3 Important Voter Rights

1 | You have the right to disability assistance.

Federal law says all polling stations must be accessible to people with disabilities. It also says it's not enough to have curbside voting available to make voting physically accessible. There needs to be a way for people with all types of disabilities to vote independently. If you have a reading disability or low vision, you have the right to ask about access to a machine that reads the ballot for you. If you're unable to write, the law also allows you to bring someone to help you while you're casting your vote.

2 | You have the right to vote early.

This is a right I've exercised when I knew I was going to be out of town on Election Day. Most states also have approved locations and dates for early voting. Where I live, I just have to go to city hall. If you're not sure where you can vote early near you, check out the comprehensive information provided for each state at Vote.org. You can also vote absentee by mail.

3 | You have the right to cast your vote on Election Day.

In some states, you can register for the first time at your polling station and vote on Election Day. In other states, you must register in advance. You may not even have to put on shoes to do it—many states will let you register online. Check out Vote.gov to find the rules for your state.

Once you're registered, you have the right to vote on Election Day. Even if the polls close while you're in line, stay in that line! They have to let you cast your vote. If the electronic machines aren't working, you have the right to ask for and use a paper ballot. And you can also ask for a new ballot if you make a mistake.

Being an Informed Voter

Being a voter is more than registering. Unless you actually vote, you're not a voter. And if you go to the polls knowing nothing about what you're voting on, you're not an informed one. I was surprised to realize the first time I voted that there was more on the ballot than candidates. There were also referendums (general votes on a single political question) and issues I had to make decisions about. Who knew? Clearly, not me. But you know now. So, here are the steps to becoming an informed voter.

1 | Register to vote.

Voter registration is different from state to state. As I said before, most states will let you register online or in person. But find out and do it. It should take you less than ten minutes.

2 | Know about the political parties.

You probably already know that the political system in the U.S. is dominated by two major political parties—the Democratic Party and the Republican Party (though there are smaller parties). You don't have to register as being part of a particular party, and even if you do, you don't have to vote for a member of that party. But it's a good idea to know what the parties are and what they tend to stand for so you can make informed decisions about registering and voting.

There's no way you've made it to adulthood without hearing about the "left" and the "right" when it comes to U.S. politics. The thing is, if you ask ten different people, you're probably going to get ten different answers about what each of them means. (You're also likely to get into some sort of argument, so be cautious with whom you have the conversation.)

Traditionally, politics have been thought of as being on a left-to-right axis, with the two major parties on either end. The Democratic Party is on the left, the Republican Party (also known as the Grand Old Party or GOP) is on the right, and independent voters are often somewhere in the middle (but not always). There are also other parties and movements, like the Green Party, the Libertarian Party, and the Tea Party movement. In most states, you only register as a Republican, Democrat, or independent voter (no party). Here's a quick look at the traditional values of each party.

- **The Democratic Party** uses a donkey as its logo, and tends to rally around issues of equality, like human rights, affordable education for all, universal healthcare, and taxation rates relative to your income.

- **The Republican Party** uses an elephant as its logo and tends to rally around issues of free enterprise and fiscal conservatism, like smaller government, free market capitalism, lower taxes, and gun ownership rights.

- **The Green Party** has been around since 2001, with four main values: social justice, nonviolence, ecological wisdom, and grassroots democracy. Don't know what ecological wisdom is? It centers on the idea that we're part of a complex ecosystem, so we have a responsibility to respect and protect biodiversity and land resources. Grassroots democracy is when political processes and decisions are driven by ordinary citizens, instead of larger organizations or wealthy individuals.

- **The Libertarian Party** is sort of a mix of the Democratic and Republican. Its focus is on maximizing personal freedom and minimizing government involvement. It's fiscally conservative, but socially liberal.

3 | Know the issues.

All states, and even cities, have issues to be voted on. They can run the range from allocating money to a school budget, to deciding on ranked choice voting, and all sorts of other issues. Do your research. Don't just read one person's opinion—seek out information about all sides of an issue. Then you can vote in a way that combines your personal values with the facts.

4 | Know your polling place.

Your polling station is based on your address, and you'll usually get a notification in the mail about where to vote. If you don't know where to go, call your local election office, or use the polling place locator on Vote.org to find, well, your polling place.

5 | Go vote!

When Your Address Changes

I lived in nine different apartments in my early-adult life. Each time I had to remember to change my address with all sorts of places, change over the utilities, and get my mail forwarded. You're going to want to do that, too. Otherwise, important notices and birthday checks may not make their way to you. It's just another mundane detail of adulting.

Updating Your Mailing Address with the USPS

The majority of getting your mail to the right place relies on you telling the United States Postal Service you've moved on. Once you do that, your mail will automatically be forwarded to your new address for six months. Mostly, at least. Some things slip by, but most of it makes it to you. You can do a change of address online at USPS.com/move for just about $1. (The cost is to verify your identity.)

Letting Others Know You've Moved

Unless you're lying low, you're going to want to let other people know of your new address, too. This is maybe one of the few times it's OK to send a mass email. Just, please, remember to put everybody's email address on bcc, not cc. Your cool, well-known friends may not appreciate you revealing their email address to your grandmother. You also need to tell:

- Your employer
- Your bank and credit card companies
- Your doctor's office
- Your car and health insurance
- Your cell phone provider
- Your favorite online shopping outlets
- Any professional organizations you belong to
- Any magazines or professional journals you receive in the mail

PROTECTING YOUR IDENTITY

You have an ID, you're a registered voter, and you have a stable address. You have an identity connected to a bunch of systems that contain a lot of personal information about you. That personal information is valuable. It's the reason that identity theft is a fast-growing cybercrime.

There are people who will steal that information to access bank accounts, take out credit cards or other lines of credit in your name, or do other criminal-type things. And a lot of us inadvertently make it easy for people to get that information, which is known as personally identifiable information (or PII). So, let's talk a little about protecting your identity.

7 Ways Your Identity Can Be Stolen

Nobody wants to think they can be a victim of identity theft. After all, you're too smart to fall for any of those email scams saying you've won or owe money, right? And you're definitely not going to get catfished because you know all the tricks for making sure someone is who they claim to be on the internet. I mean, we've all watched Nev and Max at work on MTV's *Catfish*. Unfortunately, identity theft most often occurs because of daily habits. Here are some examples:

1 | Social media.

I talked about locking down privacy settings on your social media accounts. It also plays into protecting your identity. On Facebook, identity thieves can grab your maiden name (or your mother's if she shows as a relative) and your birth date—two pieces of info commonly used as security questions to access accounts. But there are also all sorts of "games" that people play that give out tons of information. Next time you're asked to participate in a "10 Facts About Me" post on social media, look carefully at the questions. They're usually pretty close to the things you use as answers to security questions: Your favorite color, your first pet's name, the name of the street you lived on when you were a kid, etc. Feel free to be the spoilsport who doesn't cut-paste-and-share.

2 | Giving out your Social Security number.

There are plenty of times it's legit to give out your Social Security number, but usually you only need to give the last four digits to verify your identity. Be wary if you're asked for the whole number and be even warier about providing it in an email, to a non-secure website (make sure the URL has a locked padlock next to it in your browser) or to a company that called you. Instead, ask them for a number that you can call back to speak with them, so you can verify they're for real.

3 | Reusing passwords.

I'm going to assume you know better than to use "1234" or "password" as your password. I'm not going to assume you don't use the same password for multiple logins. I mean, it's hard to remember passwords, so I get it. But if there's a data breach somewhere—and it happens all the time—cybercriminals tend to connect passwords to other PII and either use it or sell it to others. In an instant, all of your accounts are at risk. So, think about investing in a password management app like LastPass instead of reusing the same old password.

4 | Throwing away mail.

I am completely guilty of this one, and tend to throw away mail that has sensitive information on it without ripping it up or shredding it first. And then I dig through the trash to find it. Bills that you pay online, credit card offers, and other mail that has any personally identifiable information on it could be discovered in a dumpster dive. (Yes, people actually do that. Ick.)

5 | Using public Wi-Fi.

If you work in airports, hotels, coffee shops, or other public places, be wary. Most public Wi-Fi is unencrypted and data can be intercepted. So, if you can, wait until you're home to log into your bank account or to buy something online. And, if you're "borrowing" your neighbor's internet, keep in mind that if you could get on their network, other people can, too.

6 | Falling for phishing.

I'm sorry to say that sometimes impersonators or people who run phishing schemes are really, really clever. They send emails that look like legitimate notifications that you need to reset your password because of a data breach. They send emails that look like they're from your Aunt Barbara. They call you and convince you they're from your credit card company. But none of that is true. If you're asked to reset a password, log into the account directly to see if the password really does need to be changed. Hover over any link in your email before you click it. (You should be able to see the URL it's taking you to, and if it looks suspicious it probably is.) Check to make sure the email is coming from Aunt Barbara's email address or text her to make sure. Ask the credit card company if you can call them back at a more convenient time, and call the number on the back of your card.

7 | Poor data protection.

Remember the internet connection you "borrowed" from your neighbor because they didn't protect their network? Don't be that neighbor. And don't be the person who has your phone, tablet, or computer available to pop onto. Password protect your devices and networks. Consider changing the password after guests leave.

How to Know If Your Identity Has Been Stolen

You have to be vigilant to make sure your identity isn't stolen. Some things to keep an eye on:

- **Bank statements.** Look for charges you don't recognize.
- **Credit cards.** Set an alert that emails or texts you every time you make a purchase. Better to be annoyed than sorry.
- **Online accounts.** Keep an eye out for unusual purchases or logins from new devices.
- **Mail.** Make sure you're still getting all the bills you should and no new ones you shouldn't.
- **Credit reports.** The three credit reporting bureaus, Experian, TransUnion, and Equifax, are required by law to each provide you with one credit report per year. That means you can get one every four months. Do it, and make sure you recognize all the accounts that are open in your name.

What to Do If Your Identity Has Been Stolen

Learning someone is using your identity can be scary and feel like a huge invasion. Stay as calm as you can and start by calling your bank, your credit card companies, and anywhere else you have an open line of credit. Tell them you think your identity has been stolen, freeze any new activity, cancel your cards, and get new ones issued. (This is where your emergency cash stash comes in handy.)

Then, log into each credit bureaus' website and put a credit freeze in place. This means no new credit lines can be taken out in your name without you being contacted and everything being verified.

Next, call the police. Identity theft is a crime. You need to file a report so that they can make sure the correct authorities are on it and to make sure there's a record of you saying, "Hey, someone stole my identity."

Lastly, call a friend or family member who you can cry all over or rant to. They've got you and will provide comfort and maybe even a loan until you get your new debit card.

You're Crushing Adulting

It can be overwhelming to take on the responsibilities of an adult. Though I've been at it a while, at least three times a week, I say to myself (or my husband if he happens to be nearby), "That's a very adult-sounding sentence," or "That's something only a real adult would have to think about." It's not something you ever really get used to, but it is something you get better at in ways that just sort of creep up on you.

Thinking about voting and how to manage letting everybody know you've moved so they can contact you are two of those ways. You've moved past the basic questions about how to afford an adult life or find a job and are thinking more globally about what it means to be an adult. That's some next-level adulting, and it's a big deal. Before you move on, take a minute to reflect on how far you've come. All kidding and snarky comments aside, I think you're starting to crush it.

6 |
TAKE CARE
Insurance and Other Healthy Stuff

It's easy to get caught up in the day-to-day work of being an adult so you forget to take care of yourself or have on hand the things you need to do that. And taking care of yourself comes in many different flavors. Some of it's having what you need to make sure your physical health doesn't suffer. Some of it's doing what you need to do to make sure your mental health doesn't suffer. And some of it's doing what you need to make sure your social life doesn't suffer. Let's talk about what it means to take care of yourself.

Taking Care of You

The other day I got a paper cut. Ironically, it was from opening the envelope of a medical bill, but that's not the point I'm trying to make. You know how paper cuts hurt really badly and with every throb of your finger, you worry that it's going to get infected and then you'll be known as the person who went to the emergency room for a paper cut? (That may just be me. I'm a baby when it comes to those things.)

Anyway…I got this paper cut and decided I was going to do the very adult thing of getting on top of the situation by washing it, putting on antibiotic ointment, and covering it with a Band-Aid. Well, I washed it, and then found the empty tube that used to have antibiotic ointment in it, and finally managed to scrounge up a Star Wars Band-Aid from our junk drawer. Not my best adult moment. By the time I found what I needed to fix it, it wasn't even throbbing anymore. What if I'd really hurt myself? Like, what if I'd gotten a cardboard cut instead? So, what did I learn from that experience? A couple of things. The first is that I clearly need to up my first-aid supply game. (Although, I did get quite a few compliments on my Yoda Band-Aid.) The second is that I need to take care of little medical things to make sure they don't turn into bigger ones. I'm passing this on so you don't have to make too many trips to the ER or doctor.

Basic First-Aid Supplies to Have

You should have a first-aid kit that is easy to find when you're burned, bleeding, or barfing. You can buy a pre-stocked one, but they tend to be expensive and come with just the absolute basics. Also, for some reason, every time I've ever tried to use anything in one of those kits, the alcohol wipes are all dried out or the bandages don't stick or something like that.

To that end, it's worth making your own. You can buy one of those sectioned tackle boxes at a dollar store if you want to make it fancy. Personally, I'm a fan of throwing everything into one of those plastic pencil cases. They latch, they don't take up too much space, and I'm not trying to figure out how to make a tube of antibiotic ointment fit into a compartment that's too small for it.

I know what I should have around the house to manage basic things like cuts, scrapes, burns, and stress headaches because this isn't my first day adulting. You, on the other hand, haven't been doing this as long, so you get a pass—and a list of the basics you should have on hand.

- **Thermometer:** In our house, we use a fancy-pants temporal one that makes me feel like I'm in a sci-fi movie. But a digital under-the-tongue one works just as well and is a lot cheaper.
- **Band-Aids**: Just make sure you have different sizes. There's nothing more frustrating in a paper-cut emergency than trying to make a large Band-Aid stick on a small finger. Or trying to cover a scraped knee with about twenty-five tiny little Band-Aids.
- **Aloe vera gel:** This is great for burns with its soothing, cooling, and moisturizing properties.
- **Antibiotic ointment:** Look for NEOSPORIN or Bacitracin, and then buy the generic version. (Don't buy hydrocortisone cream by mistake. It's great for itching, but won't keep germs from settling in.)
- **Calamine lotion or hydrocortisone cream:** Put this on hives or bug bites to make sure you don't scratch them open to the point where you need antibiotic ointment and a Band-Aid.

- **Antiseptic or alcohol wipes:** You don't have to have both on hand, but should have one or the other. You can buy rubbing alcohol or hydrogen peroxide and some cotton balls, but they're not going to fit as easily into your pencil case or tackle box.
- **Adhesive first-aid tape:** Sometimes, a Band-Aid won't do, and you need to cover a cut or burn with gauze pads. They don't stick by themselves, so have some tape on hand. And make sure it (a) tears off the roll easily and (b) doesn't tear your skin off when you remove it. There are some great paper-like tapes that will do.
- **Medical gauze pads or roll:** Rolled gauze is, well, gauzier, than gauze pads. You have to cut off a section of rolled gauze and layer it to cover a burn effectively. I recommend a box of different-sized gauze pads instead.
- **Scissors:** If you have gauze or tape that doesn't tear easily, you'll need these. You may also need to cut gum out of your hair or something, so it's good to have on hand anyway.
- **Tweezers:** For removing splinters or other things that get under your skin.
- **Acetaminophen and ibuprofen (aka Tylenol and Advil):** Stress headaches, fevers, strained muscles…need I say more?
- **Antihistamine (aka Benadryl):** You may want both pill and liquid versions. I have allergic reactions to bug bites and some foods. I carry an EpiPen, but if it's not dire, I can take liquid Benadryl, which works to calm the reaction quickly. Benadryl can cause drowsiness, so get the non-drowsy kind if necessary.
- **Disposable plastic gloves:** It's a good idea to go non-latex in case someone is helping who might be allergic. And if you're helping someone else, try to always wear the gloves so you're not in direct contact with their blood or other bodily fluids.

Always Clean the Cut

Joking aside, I needed to clean my paper cut. Anytime you have a break in your skin, it's an entryway for germs and bacteria. Wiping the blood away with a tissue or putting your finger in your mouth may take care of it on a surface level, but you need to wash the area. Soap and water work fine, or use alcohol or antiseptic wipes.

Make sure the bleeding has stopped. If it doesn't, put pressure on the area while covering it with some gauze, a paper towel, or a clean cloth. Once the bleeding subsides, put some antibiotic ointment on it—enough to cover it, but not too much that the Band-Aid slides off—and bandage it. A little oozing is to be expected, but if it outright bleeds and won't stop, it's time to take a trip to urgent care.

Mind the Burn

Many burns come from moves like picking up a pot that's still hot, trying to take muffins out of the pan before they cool, or spending too much time in the sun. As soon as you can, get cold water or ice on the area, and then put some aloe vera gel or antibiotic ointment on it. You can also take ibuprofen or acetaminophen for pain relief.

That is, assuming it's a first-degree burn (red and painful) or second-degree burn (red, painful, and blistered a little bit). Beyond that, you're going to want to talk to urgent care again. Here's a good rule of thumb: If you know you burned yourself, you can see you've burned yourself because the skin looks white or blistered, but it doesn't hurt, seek care.

When to Go to the Doctor

It took me a long time to learn that wait and see isn't a good healthcare strategy. I waited and saw myself into too many colds-turned-bronchitis before I realized it's smarter to see the doctor and find out you didn't need to than to not see the doctor and realize you really should have.

Make the appointment if you're feeling persistently unwell. You may have to talk to a nurse who will help decide if you should come in, but you're still talking to a medical professional with a better grasp than you on what's going around, what needs to be looked at, and what can be taken care of at home. If the reason you need to see the doctor feels personal, say that. "I prefer to talk to somebody in person. I'm not comfortable going into detail on the phone." You'll probably have to give a general overview, such as "It's about my mental health," or "I'm having some issues with sexual health," or "I found a lump that worries me."

Health Insurance and Adulting

I'm going to say it again—accidents and illnesses happen, and they don't care how old you are. I have more friends than I can count who thought they didn't need health insurance when they first started their adult lives and are still drowning in medical debt because of it. Insurance can be the best invisible thing you own. But getting it can be a hassle.

Finding and Choosing Health Insurance

If you're lucky, you have a job that provides health insurance. If you're even luckier, you live in a country that provides universal healthcare (there are still challenges, but insurance isn't one).

Let's assume you live in a country that doesn't have universal healthcare. Even if your employer provides health insurance, you usually still have to pay for some of it, as well as some medical costs, but it will save you money. My friend's husband's salary is about the same amount as what they pay for child care, but he keeps the job so they can have insurance. It's all about the trade-off.

If you don't have employer-provided health insurance, and you live in the U.S., you can visit the U.S. Department of Health & Human Services' marketplace at Healthcare.gov to purchase a plan that works for you and your budget. Regardless of whether you do it through the marketplace or work, figuring out which healthcare plan to choose is enough to make your mind melt. Every year, I look at the options and cry. Seriously, sitting at my desk bawling because I can't figure out how I'm smart enough to have a job, but not smart enough to make sense of the implications of each plan.

What's an HMO?

HMO stands for *health maintenance organization*. If you have an HMO, you may pay less for health insurance, but to avoid paying a ton out of your own pocket when you get care, the provider (the doctor or facility you're using) has to be in the HMO's approved network of providers that take your insurance. You typically have a primary care provider (PCP, your main physician for regular checkups, etc.), and if you need to see a specialist, your PCP will have to make a referral or the specialist visit won't be covered. An HMO means you're limited in your ability to choose your PCP or other providers, but it's typically less expensive. It's also usually pretty easy to log into your plan's website to see which providers are in the network, so that you can choose where to go for care, especially for routine checkups and office visits.

What's a PPO?

PPO stands for *preferred provider organization*. Like an HMO, it has an approved network of providers that charge a reduced fee for the PPO members. You don't usually need a referral to see in an in-network healthcare provider, and you can even see those who don't belong to the network. Let's say, for example, you had a doctor you loved before you got a job with insurance, and now that doctor isn't in the network. You can still use them; it's just going to cost more. Your insurance company keeps a list of all the in-network care providers online, so you can check before making an appointment.

What's an HDHP?

HDHP is a *high-deductible health plan*. You pay a higher deductible (more on that soon), but you also pay less monthly for the plan (that cost is your "premium"). So, you may pay a small premium, but much more out of pocket when you do need healthcare. If you're in good health without ongoing medical needs, this is a good way to go.

What's an HSA?

HSA stands for *health savings account*. With an HSA through your employer, you have money taken out of your paycheck pre-tax and set aside in an account to pay costs not covered by insurance. Lots of people who have an HDHP also have an HSA. The money stays in your account, doesn't get taxed, and can be used for expenses like copayments (set amounts for doctor visits, prescriptions, etc.), deductibles (see below), hospital costs, etc. Your HSA will have a list of what qualifies.

Deductibles and Out-of-Pocket Costs

If you have a choice of plans, you need to decide whether to pay a higher monthly premium to avoid paying a lot out of pocket toward your deductible (how much you must pay out of your own pocket in a year before insurance starts to pay—and you don't have to pay anymore that year), or a lower monthly premium with a lower out-of-pocket deductible. The dilemma is having to come up with the money up front. Is it worth it to pay more monthly in order to make sure I don't end up in a spot where I need care and don't have the money to pay for it? Figuring out which will cost more in the end is mind-bending because you can't predict all future healthcare needs. You can, however, know how much you need to pay for some things, like regular prescriptions. Many plans have two deductibles—the amount you must pay toward care and the amount you must pay toward prescriptions.

How Does a Deductible Work?

Insurance protects you against future risk. If something happens to you, the insurance company will help you out financially. They're all in for that, but want to know you'll help, too. If your deductible is $1000, you're saying, "I know I have to pay $1000 before you come to the rescue and pay the rest." The lower your deductible, the higher your monthly premium is likely to be. The insurance company is like, "Cool, you only have to pay $100 before we come to the rescue, but we need more money up front."

Is My Deductible Always a Set Amount?

Not necessarily. Some are a set amount. Others may be a percentage of the cost of the visit. For instance, you may have to cover 20% of your hospital stay and the insurance will pay the rest.

Does Everything I Pay Count toward My Deductible?

No. Most of the time, copayments are excluded. You must pay that amount for every office visit or prescription, no matter what.

What Happens When I Meet My Deductible?

On most plans, once you meet your yearly deductible, you don't pay any more out-of-pocket costs (until the next calendar year).

Picking a Plan

Picking the right health insurance plan often relies on predicting health issues you may experience in the next year, some of which are predictable and some which are not. Questions to consider:

1. Can you afford the monthly premium?
If you're going to pay so much in insurance that you don't have enough money left to pay your bills, it's not the right plan for you.

2. How often do you go to the doctor now?
If you're a generally healthy human who doesn't go to the doctor that often, it may be worth paying a lower premium and a higher copay. If you catch every bug that goes around or are accident-prone, it's better to choose a higher premium plan with a lower copay.

3. Do you have a preexisting condition that requires specialized care, medications, or medical equipment?
Choose a plan that covers the equipment you need, the prescriptions you take, and that will allow you to see specialists with a low copay. It may mean a higher premium, but in the end you'll pay less.

4. Do you want to keep a specific healthcare provider?
If your provider is in-network, no problem. If not, choose a plan that allows you to go out-of-network without high copays.

5. If you get sick or injured, what's the most you would have to pay out-of-pocket?
This is where the guesswork comes in. But, assume you have a bad accident, get cancer, or get COVID-19. If the amount you'd have to pay before your insurance kicks in is exorbitant, it may be worth paying a higher premium up front.

Choosing a Primary Care Provider

Now that you've got your health insurance figured out, you can do the very grown-up thing of picking your own primary care provider (PCP). This is usually your primary doctor; but it could be a nurse practitioner or a practice comprised of many doctors and nurses. What it can't be is your pediatrician (a doctor specializing in kids that you may have been seeing most of your life so far). My daughter got fired by her pediatrician when she was nineteen. She hadn't picked a new doctor, so the health insurance company picked one for her, transferred her records, and she was stuck with somebody she didn't choose (though you can change your PCP later). Here are some things to consider when finding a PCP:

- **Is the provider part of your insurance network?** You can look up providers on the health insurance website and filter them to within a certain number of miles near your zip code.

- **Did somebody you know (and trust) recommend them?** It's hard to pick a doctor from a list of names. Ask around and see who your friends use. If nobody has a recommendation, at least check the reviews online before making an appointment.

- **Did you get a good vibe when you called to set up an initial appointment?** The attitude of the reception staff is usually a good reflection of the type of care you'll get from the office.

- **Was it easy to get an appointment?** If the provider books out weeks ahead, you may want to ask how long it would take you to get an appointment if you're sick or injured.

- **Do you feel listened to?** You have to be your own healthcare advocate (that whole communicating thing). If you don't feel listened to, you can't be an effective advocate.

Keep in mind that you can always change doctors. It may be

uncomfortable, but if you don't like your doctor or feel good about the care you're getting, there's nothing wrong with asking for your records and transferring to a new doctor. In fact, it's a very grown-up move.

HEALTHY HABITS FOR MENTAL HEALTH

Adulting is exciting, but it can be legitimately stressful. And somehow you have to find healthy ways to manage that stress.

1 | Know that you're going to feel bad sometimes.

You know what I really dislike? When someone says, "Oh, just don't worry about it." You know what I outright hate? When someone says to me, "Stop crying. You need to try to feel better."

Strong emotions make some people uncomfortable, but nobody ever stopped worrying because they were told not to. Sometimes you don't need to try to feel better. Sometimes, what you need to do is give yourself over to the worry and bad feelings in order to get through them.

Accept that you're going to feel sad, angry, frustrated, or some other unpleasant emotion. Not everything needs to be fixed. Sometimes things need to run their course, and it's healthy to allow yourself to feel a full range of emotions. Feeling negative emotions can often be the thing that spurs you to make change so you can feel better. If you ignore them, it's harder to find out what's behind them.

Give up acting like you've always got it together all the time. Be vulnerable. Be emotional. Let it work its way through your system, and acknowledge that a constant state of happiness isn't the way to live a full and fulfilling life.

2 | Find somebody to talk to.

OK, we've established that it's totally normal to feel overwhelmed, discouraged, or sad at times. But if that's your baseline state, it's time to pay more attention to your mental health. Not being able to "push through" depression or anxiety isn't a character flaw. It's a sign you may need additional support to feel better and get to a place where you can be a more successful adult. Mental health issues are common, and there are people who can help.

Talk with your healthcare provider if you're feeling unable to shake worry, anxiety, sadness, or other paralyzing feelings. They may suggest you try talk therapy or a combination of therapy and medication. There is no shame or weakness in doing either or both. You just have to be willing to put in the work. (And if you're nervous about talking to a healthcare provider you may not know very well yet about your mental health, it's OK to reach out to other people to help you navigate things. Part of being an adult is knowing that in some cases, it's absolutely fine to lean on parents, other family members, or friends, if you know they will be supportive.)

A therapist or counselor can see your life in a way you can't when you're in the thick of it. Having a neutral somebody to talk to and help you find ways to cope with the daily stressors of adulting can be amazingly helpful. They'll be able to help you think through small (and big) things you can do to feel better so that you can eventually make choices to help you feel in control again. I know from experience that anxiety and depression can trick you into thinking there aren't solutions, ways to feel better, or that you don't have any control over or choice in how your life unfolds. That's not true, and knowing you're not alone really helps! And if you're concerned about someone else's mental health, there's nothing wrong with letting them know you're concerned and are willing to help if you can.

3 | Make the time to exercise.

I exercise, but only when it occurs to me that I need to. It's not built into my routine, even though I know I feel better mentally when I'm exercising regularly. Don't be me. You can build this habit early in your life. You don't have to join a gym or go to spin class or hot yoga (unless you want to and can afford it). Exercise can take many forms. Go for walks. Take up running. Follow along with YouTube workouts (like The Fitness Marshall videos) when nobody is around to watch you.

Research shows exercise has huge benefits on your mental well-being. People who exercise regularly have more energy, they sleep better, they feel less stressed, and their mood is better. It also helps improve memory (another finding that makes me think I really need to start doing it more often).

4 | Manage your time as well as you can.

I know, I know. You read this and rolled your eyes so hard you sprained one. Time management is something we all talk about when we're all talking about how busy we are. What we don't talk about is how to do it. When you're first starting out your adult life, there's this weird pressure to prove you can do it all and not buckle under the weight of it. I am here to tell you two things:

- You can't do it all and do it all well at the same time.
- Successful people don't do it all; they figure out what's worth doing, what's worth losing, and then prioritize what's left.

President Eisenhower apparently said, "What is important is seldom urgent, and what is urgent is seldom important." The Eisenhower Matrix of time management is a decision-making framework for prioritizing things by Do, Decide, Delegate, or Delete the things on your plate.

Do, Decide, Delegate, or Delete

The Eisenhower Matrix of time management is a decision-making framework that helps prioritize things by urgency and importance.

Do
Do it now. These are things that are time-sensitive and need to be done immediately.

Decide
Schedule a time to do it. These are things you need to prioritize and schedule time to do.

Delegate
Can someone else do it? These are things that are urgent, but that someone else can handle.

Delete
Eliminate it. These are things that are neither urgent nor important and are a waste of your time.

5 | Make time for friends and fun.

You're in a place in your life where you can finally make your own decisions, do what you want (as long as it's not illegal or harmful), and enjoy your life. So, make a habit of having fun with friends. It doesn't have to be elaborate, expensive, or even often, but friendship and laughter are such an important part of being healthy. Just having one good friend to spend some time with can make the difference between a good day and a bad one.

If you're in a new place and haven't made friends yet, make time to connect with an old one, such as having virtual coffee or drinks with a faraway friend. Start a text chain that is specifically to send jokes or memes. Or, start a text chain that can be used to keep your friend group up to date on what's happening in each other's' lives. You're worth it and you matter.

7 |
LIVING
SITUATIONS
Rent, Roommates, and Reality

Let's assume you have your budget up and running, and you're in one of a few transition places in your life. That often means you're going to be looking for a place to live. That's exciting! Finding an apartment, buying a house, choosing a roommate—those are among the things that make you feel like a capital "G" Grown-up.

You're Finishing up School

Take a moment to pause. This is a huge moment in your life that comes with a range of emotions—fear, excitement, sadness, pride, and perhaps a sudden desire to go to graduate school to delay this transition. I'm proud of you, and I don't even know you. You've done a big thing and are moving on to a totally new phase of your life. Don't underestimate the enormity of that accomplishment or of the weird roller coaster of feelings you're going to have as you hunt for housing.

It's Best to Part Ways With a Roommate or Partner

If this is a breakup-related housing search, make sure to read this carefully. You may want to get out of there as soon as possible, but jumping into a lousy housing situation for the sake of expedience isn't going to make you feel better.

The first time I got married, I was young. Well, that means that in my early adulting years, I moved out of a house I never should have bought in the first place, and into my own apartment. That apartment was the last bad choice I made before I started living my best adult life. I panic-signed a lease before thinking through whether the place I chose was right for me in that time in my life.

Your Lease Is Up on the Miserable Apartment You're Living in Now

Maybe the place is less than ideal because you took the first one you could find, didn't do your research, or couldn't afford anything better. The good news is, if your place is miserable because you didn't do the research or panic-signed a lease, you probably won't make the same mistake again.

You're Living with Family, but It's Time to Find Your Own Place

We're all aware of the memes and snarky jokes about adult children living with their parents, but just to be clear, for some people it works really well. What gets lost in the midst of that snark is that there's a big difference between living with your parents and living off of your parents. If you're there to help take care of the house or family members, and are meaningfully contributing to the household in a way that's working for all of you, forget what anybody else has to say about it. But of course, sometimes it's just time...

The Hidden Costs of Apartment Living

Just like there are hidden costs when it comes to your budget, there are hidden costs of housing. It would be simple if the monthly rent were the only thing you had to think about when you look at an apartment. But it's not. It's like when you buy a computer or a car and you're like, "I can totally afford this one!" And then the salesperson tells you that's the base price, and if you want any software or, in the case of a car, air conditioning or to pick the color, the costs keep adding up. And while maybe you don't need the specific, costly virus-protection software for your computer, and you're cool with taking the car in white because it's the one they have on the lot, there are some things you have no choice about paying extra for.

Let's bring this back to the costs of housing. Even if they don't all apply to you right now, stay with me. At the very least, you'll get to be the person in your friend group who can ask, "Hey, but did you think about…? Once you're living in an apartment, your rent will be pretty much locked in for the duration of the lease. It's the costs that come with a new apartment that you have to think through.

Security Deposit

Security deposits vary depending on the landlord or real estate management company, but it's standard to pay your first month's rent plus a security deposit of another month's rent before you move in. Some places expect a security deposit of up to a month's rent, plus first and last month's rent before you move in. That can be a ton of money, especially if you live in a big city or a place where apartments are scarce. For example, when a friend moved from his Brooklyn apartment to a one-bedroom studio in midtown Manhattan, the amount he had to put down just to get the key was equivalent to about six months of what I pay for my three-bedroom townhouse in the suburbs of Portland, Maine.

Application and Paperwork Fees

Landlords, especially those who own multiple properties, and real estate management companies tend to run both background and credit checks on potential tenants. That costs them money, and a lot of the time you actually end up paying for it yourself through an application fee. Ask them what the application fee is for and whether you'll get it back. In some states, if you don't get the place, the landlord is required to refund your fee. If you do get the place, some may also deduct that fee from the deposit you'll pay. And don't forget to ask what other apartments they have too, so you can make your application fee go farther.

Renter's Insurance

The idea of something happening to your stuff or your apartment before you even move in can be a downer, but is also a totally adult move. Landlords have property and liability insurance, but if something happens, be it a natural disaster or a break-in, that insurance only covers the dwelling. Renter's insurance is a policy you pay for that covers your personal property in case something happens to it. Some landlords have a clause in the lease that says you must have renter's insurance.

I'd never been so happy to have paid for an insurance policy than when we lost power for a week the day after I went grocery shopping. Our insurance actually covered the cost of all the food we lost. And there was also the time there was a small flood in our basement storage space due to a sudden spring thaw while there was still close to two feet of snow on the ground. Hooray for renter's insurance!

Appliances

Does your dream apartment come with a washer and dryer? Or just a hookup for a washer and dryer? If you only have the hookup, you're probably looking at laundromat costs, unless you have the money to buy appliances. But they're expensive. I knew I was a true adult the day I started looking at the sale prices on stackable washer-dryer combos instead of clothes. It was a very grown-up moment.

Utilities

What's included in rent varies from place to place. Some complexes and buildings include utilities in the rent, while others don't. (For example, you pay rent, but you also have to pay for heat on top of that). While water, sewer and trash are commonly included, it's important to know what's included with your rent and what's not. Read the apartment listings carefully, and also follow up by asking landlords or property managers when you view an apartment (more on that later). It's important, because utilities like heat can be costly, especially in places with cold winters. So you'll need to factor that in.

WHAT ABOUT HOMEOWNERSHIP?

You may consider buying your own home, and I don't want to discourage you from doing so if you have the money (which will not only include a down payment on a loan, but also inspection fees, closing costs, homeowner's insurance, property taxes, etc.). Also keep in mind that when you own a home, you are responsible for all maintenance, whether you do the work yourself or you pay someone else to do it. And if you're starting out in a career that you may end up moving for, selling a house can be a little more complicated than moving out of an apartment. That doesn't mean you shouldn't consider it if you can manage the costs. If you can put some money down and get a good interest rate, you mortgage payment and taxes may end up being less than you'd pay for rent, and probably for more space. A home is also an investment for which you acquire equity (the value of the home minus what you owe on it). There are definitely pros and cons to both renting and buying.

Pros and Cons of Renting vs. Owning

PROS of Renting
- No down payment (but you usually need to pay a deposit)
- Low or no maintenance costs
- Short-term commitment, easy to move
- No property taxes

CONS of Renting
- Less privacy, must deal with landlord or management company
- No equity or buildup of wealth
- Rent can increase over time
- Building rules, regulations, and limitations

PROS of Owning
- More privacy
- Tax credits and building equity (it's an investment)
- Fixed payments
- You can personalize; it's yours!

CONS of Owning
- Expensive, requires a lot of money up front
- Inspection fees, closing costs
- Homeowner's insurance and property taxes
- Utility bills (the bigger the house, the higher the bills)
- Maintenance and repair costs
- Big commitment, less flexibility to move

FINDING YOUR OWN PLACE

Apartment hunting and imagining your life in a new place can be fun, but it can also be exhausting, especially if it's one of the first times you're doing it or you have a tight budget. I know because I've had a lot of experience doing it. In the first couple decades of my adult life, I lived in no fewer than nine apartments. Why so often? I moved a few times for schooling and career reasons. But I also moved more than a few times because I didn't do enough research (to make sure my landlord wasn't planning on selling the building, or would actually pay to make sure the furnace wouldn't run out of heating oil in the dead of the winter, etc.).

Where to Search for Apartments

I've always found even just figuring out where to find places to look at is an ordeal. Maybe some of that is because I started that process when you still had to search for apartment listings in an

4 Apartment Hunting Sites and Apps

- **APARTMENTS.COM** is the top apartment listing website. On any given day, renters can access details about more than a million available apartments across the nation. It has a team of researchers that visits properties to save you the time of doing some of the legwork.

- **ZILLOW** has an app and a website. You can personalize your settings not only for searching, but also so that you can get alerts when something that matches your preferences is available.

- **ZUMPER** is an app and website you can use to search for rental houses, rooms, condos, or apartments. You can fill out rental applications through the app, and they update regularly, so you don't waste your time looking at places that aren't available.

- **RENT.COM** is for both tenants and landlords. You can search by a number of criteria, and look at photos, floor plans, ratings, and reviews before deciding to contact anybody.

actual newspaper or ask friends if they knew of anything. (That last one is still a good idea. You may have a friend whose apartment complex or management company offers a discount on rent to both them and you if they bring you in as new tenant.)

The internet is an awesome way to find apartment listings (newspaper classified ads are now online). Facebook and Craigslist have apartment listings, and there are other websites for apartment hunters, too.

QUESTIONS TO ASK YOURSELF BEFORE A VIEWING

If you've given yourself enough lead time, you will have the luxury of not having to take the absolute first apartment you find and to think through what you're looking for. You know what? Actually, it's probably good just to think these things through even if you're living somewhere you love. Better to know what you want before you need to know.

What Are Your Must-Haves?

Remember how when you were making a budget you looked at the difference between wants and needs? This is similar. Must-haves are nonnegotiable, and will differ person to person, depending on your individual needs. For instance, if you're disabled, accessibility in every part of the apartment complex is a must-have.

If you don't have a car, and rely on public transportation, then being close enough to walk to a bus stop or train station might be a must-have. And it may mean that onsite laundry facilities are a must-have as well.

Most of the time, must-haves include things like having the amount of space you can stand to live in, and the rent and utilities adding up to less than the maximum amount of money you can afford to spend. Personally, I'd add an elevator to my must-have list. Just the idea of carrying groceries up flights and flights of stairs makes me tired.

What Are Your Would-Be-Nices?

Then there are your would-be-nices, which are similar to your wants. These are things you would really like to have, but would give up if you found a place that you liked that had all of your must-haves. This might include things like a dishwasher, hardwood floors, a dedicated parking spot, or proximity to your favorite coffee shop or best friend.

What's the Neighborhood Like?

Check it out on Google Maps before setting a time to look at the apartment. What's nearby? How does the building look? If it passes muster online, take a look during the day—and maybe even at night. The whole point is to figure out if you feel comfortable, so I suppose if you don't feel comfortable going back at night, you already have your answer.

Check out who and what you see in the community. Are people friendly? Too friendly? Is anybody around your age? Are there places within walking distance for basic services or middle-of-the-night munchies?

What Do You Know about the Landlord?

Not all landlords or management companies are equal. A bad landlord can make your life a living hell. Do some research. If you're working with a real estate agent, ask them what they know about the landlord. And pay attention to the little things.

If you've been trying to get in touch with the landlord to see the apartment and they don't answer your calls or emails, that doesn't bode well for getting a speedy reply when you're living there, and the glass shower door falls on top of you in the middle of your morning shower. (This is a true story. The end of the story is, "and I moved out of there as soon as I could.") Remember, too, that the internet is awesome. Are there reviews online? What do they say, and what kinds of responses have been given to negative reviews?

QUESTIONS TO ASK YOURSELF DURING A VIEWING

You found a couple places to look at. Great! Now you have the task of going through a series of questions as you tour. This set is the equivalent to what I would call inside thoughts as opposed to out-loud thoughts.

Do You Feel Safe?

It isn't just about the neighborhood or the people in it. It's also things like whether there's adequate lighting when you come home at night. Or whether it's a secure building with a doorman that buzzes you in, or if it has a secure entry you have to unlock. I once lived in an idyllic neighborhood in an old Victorian house renovated as a duplex. My neighbors were friendly; there was great lighting, good parking...all the things that make you feel safe. But the neighbors who lived in the house behind ours had two vicious, scary, mean dogs and no fence. These dogs charged anybody anytime they could. I had to literally park as close as I could to my quaint Victorian porch, steel myself, and run from my car to my door to avoid those dogs. The feeling of safety was a fail.

What's Your Gut Feeling on the Person Showing You the Place?

Are they willing to answer questions? Are they a little too eager? Disgruntled? Overly cheery? Trust your instincts. If you see another tenant, feel free to ask their impressions of the place and management.

What's the Sound Situation?

My city friends tell me it's too quiet in the suburbs, but when I'm in a city, I can't stand the sound of traffic, sirens, and construction. To each their own. You're also going to want to see if you can hear your neighbors through the walls. If you can, they'll be able to hear you, and sometimes that can be super awkward. So, listen hard, and think through what you're going to be able to live with.

Is Everything Up-To-Date Enough?

Unless you're renting a brand-new unit, it's unlikely everything will be top of the line. Yet, it doesn't mean you should settle for a place without working, modern appliances. Check out the stove and refrigerator to make sure they work. Make sure all the locks actually lock and anything that should open (door, window, etc.) opens and closes. Check the heat, air conditioning (if there is any), light switches, outlets, and plumbing. How do you check outlets? Bring your phone charger, and plug it into every outlet to check to see if your phone will charge.

What About the Water?

Check the water pressure and hot water. How long does it take to get hot? How quickly does it turn cold? You don't want to have to time your showers to make sure you don't end up rinsing off in ice-cold water.

Are the Apartment, Complex, and Grounds Well Kept?

This is pretty self-explanatory. Clean is good. Dusty, dirty, dingy, scraggly, or unkempt are not good signs if the property has been deemed ready to show. I'm not one to judge anyone by the state of their lawn and gardens (or, if I'm being honest, their bathroom), but I am one to judge by the debris they leave when they want to make a good impression.

Are There Enough Outlets and Lights? Thermostat?

Assuming all the outlets work, are there enough to provide power for all your things? Are they in the right places? If you don't have any outlets in the place you'd put a workspace, it's going to be hard to charge your devices, and it may be really hard to run extension cords all over your apartment. Not to mention, it could really ruin your aesthetic. And if there are no overhead lights, you're going to have to sacrifice some of those outlets to lamps. These things are worth paying attention to. If you don't, you may end up like me the winter after we moved, searching for a thermostat to turn on the heat in my son's room, only to find there wasn't one. I mean, we got one installed, but not only was it inconvenient, it was really cold until we could get the electrician out.

Is There Enough Closet Space?

Do not assume an apartment has closets. Some old houses and buildings don't, because they were built when people had fewer clothes and pieces of furniture called wardrobes. (A wardrobe is a freestanding closet. You can still buy them, but they're expensive and take up space in your apartment.) Don't settle for less than one closet. Or two if you have a roommate or a partner you'd like to keep. Sharing a closet is rough.

Are You Going to Be Able to Move All Your Stuff In?

Take stock of the furniture you have, measure it, and bring the measurements with you. Visualize your stuff. Can it get into the apartment easily? Will it all fit? If you're like me, and you just can't see that, you can always ask the landlord for the room dimensions, and then figure it out at home later.

QUESTIONS TO ASK OUT LOUD DURING A VIEWING

Once you've gone through your "inside-thought" questions, and been silent long enough to make the person showing you the place a little nervous, it's time to ask your "out-loud-thought" questions. If you already hate the place based on the answers to your internal dialogue, it's fair to say you can skip these.

Will the Landlord Provide You with References?

It's pretty likely you'll have to provide the landlord with references if you decide you want the apartment (more on this later). It's OK to ask the landlord for references, too. Are there current or past tenants they can put you in touch with? Privacy laws may prevent them from giving out other people's info, but you can ask for somebody that might be willing to speak with you.

When Is the Place Available?

If you like to do research ahead of time, it's possible the place you're looking at doesn't have an opening right now. Ask when they anticipate having one, or, if they don't know, ask them to let you know when someone gives notice that they won't be renewing their lease. But don't put any money down to "reserve" the next apartment if there's not a firm date of when that would be available for you.

Ideally, you'll find a place to move into on exactly the first day of the month, so you don't need to pay prorated rent. That's not always the case, since once the old tenant moves out, the place should be cleaned and maybe even repainted before new tenants move in. Let the landlord know when you'll be able to move in, and see if they can work something out.

How Much Will You Have to Put Down?

This goes back to the whole security-deposit thing. You need to ask. But make sure you don't ask it in a leading way. Saying, "Do you need first and last month's rent in addition to a security deposit?" is more likely to get an enthusiastic "Yes!" than if you simply ask, "How much would I need to put down to secure the rental?"

What's Included in the Rent?

Remember that when you did your budget, you had to account for utilities? Imagine if the majority of the utilities aren't included in the rent. It would be awful to move into the best apartment ever only to discover you're paying double with heat and electric not included. Ask what's included in the rent, and then do some calculations to see if it's worth paying more than you expected in rent if you won't have to pay utilities on top of it. That said, be sure that by "included," the landlord doesn't mean, "I pay for this and will pass the charge onto you each month, so your rent is going to fluctuate depending on your utility usage." Instead it should be, "I've factored in the cost, and this flat rate accounts for what I'm paying on your behalf."

Are Pets Allowed?

If you have a pet, you're already adult enough to take care of yourself and another living being. But some apartments either don't allow animals or charge additional fees if you have one. Totally worth asking before you commit to a place before you know if Fluffy can join you.

What Cosmetic Changes Can You Make?

Most places have white walls, which they will let you paint as long as you return them to their sterile white state before you move out. Other places absolutely won't let you do that. And they won't let you put holes in the walls to hang pictures or art either. (Having seen one too many adhesive hooks pull the paint off the wall upon removal, I think landlords are missing the boat on that one, but it's not my decision to make.)

Who Do You Call If Something Breaks?

Do you call the landlord or management company when the refrigerator starts making a sound like a wheezing hippopotamus? Is there a maintenance company or technicians you call directly? In addition to knowing these things, make sure you know what the response time on maintenance requests is and what's categorized as an emergency versus a standard repair.

Don't Be Afraid to Take Your Time

Unless you're absolutely sure this is the place you want to call home, and you know it will be snapped up the minute you walk away, don't be afraid to take a day or two to think it over, especially if you have to pay an application fee. Don't pay for an application for a place you're not thrilled about.

What Are the Terms of the Lease?

You're going to want to go over the lease carefully to understand the terms, but there are some basic things to find out up front. How long is the lease for? How much notice do you need to give before you decide to renew or not? More importantly, find out how much notice the landlord has to give if they want you to move out. What you need to know about that is whether everyone is bound to the same time frame or if there are circumstances in which you may find yourself in need of moving with only thirty-days' notice.

It happens. It's why my friend had to pay a small fortune for his new place. The landlord of his old place sold the building. The new owner canceled everyone's lease and sold the building to a parking lot developer.

Whose Name Needs to Be on the Lease?

If you live with roommates, check to see if all your names must be on the lease, which is often the case. However, if that's not required, then whoever signs the lease is responsible for paying the rent. In either case, what happens if one of you chooses to move out? The flip side of this is finding out what you need to do if you move into a place that's already in someone else's name (subletting) or if you want a new roommate to move in.

The Dreaded Credit and Background Checks

Does the idea of someone doing background and credit checks on you make you feel a little sick and sweaty? I don't recommend stammering out some story about the time you didn't pay a bill and it got reported to the credit bureau because they didn't have the right address and you didn't get the bill until it was too late. I would never be so awkward as to do that the first time I met a landlord before they even asked about a credit check. And I don't have an unfounded fear a background check will dig up some crime I didn't commit, even though I know I'm a law-abiding citizen that has passed every background check ever. (OK, this *may* tie into the previous discussion of minding your mental health.)

Here's the deal, though. Weird worries aside, if it's part of the application process, you're going to have to go through the background checks. If you don't have much of a credit history yet or know your credit isn't great, you may want to say something up front, such as, "You may find my credit score is a little lower than you'd like it to be. I'm working on improving it. In the meantime, I can provide you references and am happy to show proof of income if it would help you make a decision."

That gives you a chance to give references from employers, professors, or previous landlords. It's a good way to show you're connected to the community, you understand the importance of being a good citizen, and that you're thinking ahead to make sure you can pay your rent.

So, You Think You Need a Roommate

Some people have super-discerning taste when it comes to roommates. They stick to living with people they already know and have fun with. For lots of people, that works. But keep in mind that sometimes it backfires. Your friend might be totally fun when you go out together and is a great text buddy, but have unbearable living habits or would rather spend money on concert tickets than rent. You really need to weigh whether it's worth the possibility of losing a great friendship to live with them. If you're a person like me, who doesn't particularly need to be around other people, and gets a little antsy when I feel like I have to be around them, you may be better off finding a roommate that you don't know as well.

Finding a Not-So-Terrible Roommate

That's not to say you should move in with a total stranger—you definitely need to have some sort of screening or criteria in place. So, let's figure out how to find a not-so-terrible roommate.

1 | Scroll through your contacts.

The cool thing about smartphones is that you have easy access to anyone you've ever talked to, emailed with, connected to on LinkedIn, or liked and/or friended on social media. Not all of them are going to be close friends, and some of them may even be looking for a new place to live, too. Scroll through feeds with an eye for who might be relocating or is looking for a new place to live. If you're moving to a new city, you can also check with contacts there to see if they know of anyone looking to share a place. Having a preexisting connection or mutual friend can give you some inside intel, so you're not starting from scratch.

2 | Start asking friends.

If you're not sure about living with a friend, make this a broader, more casual query. That's more, "Hey, do you know of anyone who is looking for a roommate or needs a place to live?"

3 | Interview people.

Do not offer space to the first person you talk to. Just don't do it. And don't meet them at the apartment until you're sure of them.

Go to a coffee shop, so you can get a read on them before they know where you live.

The Roommate Agreement

- Eat only food that you have bought or agreed is fair game.
- Wash your own dishes.
- Respect quiet hours.
- Give notice if you need the place for romance.
- Stick to your own parking spot.
- Pay your share of the bills, on time.
- Clean your hair out of the drain and toothpaste globs out of the sink.
- Buy (and use) your own toiletries.
- Replace the toilet paper roll.
- No, your significant other can't just crash here.

4 | Ask the right questions.

It may be great that you're both Geminis or that you have similar tastes in clothing, but what you really need to know is:

- **What do they do for a living?** You want to know if they work regularly, make enough money to pay half the bills, and if their work happens in or outside the home. If you're both working from home, even just part of the time, it may be challenging.
- **How does their lifestyle and personality compare to yours?** I love my sister, but I spent four days in a hotel room with her when she came to a conference I was speaking at, and, introvert that I am, I ended up telling her I needed her to stop narrating

everything she was doing. It wasn't my best moment. But it was too much for me to process. And that was only four days.

- **Why are they looking for a place to live?** This isn't about prying into the juicy gossip of someone else's life but more about trying to sort out whether they've been ousted by previous roommates for some egregious reason. I mean, they're probably not going to tell you that up front, but you'll get a sense of whether their story is on the up-and-up. If you're not entirely sure, ask if you can contact their last roommate for a reference.

5 | Get references.

You could stalk social media profiles, but that only gives you a sense of public persona. (But if their public persona is a jackass, I wouldn't hold out hope that their private one is all that different.) Ask for references that are not family. A former landlord or roommate, a co-worker or a friend can all provide some insights.

6 | Create a roommate agreement.

Once you've found someone to live with, put the basics in writing. You don't need to create a bathroom schedule or anything like that, but at the very least, you need to be clear about expenses and how they'll be paid. Who is giving whom half of the rent, by what date, and by what means? If the internet is in your name, do you want your roommate to pay half to your provider directly or Venmo you the money before you have to pay the bill? Then there are other things that can make or break the deal, like rules around food and the authorized (or unauthorized) eating of it. Guidelines around bringing someone home for the night. Things like that. (Yet another reason living with friends and family can be tricky. Do you want your sister or bestie to know your hookup mistakes?)

Getting Your Utilities Sorted

As much as there are things about being an adult I dislike, there are things I excel at and kind of geek out on. Playing utility Tetris is one of those things. That's when you figure out how to get the utilities turned off and out of your name at your old place long enough to make it through moving day and on at your new place in time for the day you move in. You're going to want to have your heat, electricity, and, of course, Wi-Fi, ready to go the day you move in. But some of those require a technician to come out and get them set up.

Basic Home Utilities

Once you know the terms of your lease, you'll know which utilities you need to put in your name to get up and running. Sometimes you don't have to have it turned on, but you do need to switch the account to your name from that of the previous tenant. Just be sure to ask for a totally new account number so you're not liable for any charges they may have skipped out on. The most common ones to consider:

- Electricity
- Heat (oil or natural gas)
- Cable (if you want it)
- Internet
- Water and sewer

How to Set Up Utilities

Figure out who the providers are in your new area. If there's more than one, do research into the best deals. Some cable and internet companies offer great prices for new accounts. The catch is that the introductory price is only in effect for six months to a year. Ask questions and read the fine print so you can compare based on the full price, not just the deal.

Give your utility companies a call as soon as you know you're moving and ask them how much notice they need to get things up and running. It actually works best to flat out say, "I'm moving, and I need to make the magical switchover happen on this date." And as long as you're nice to the person on the phone, they'll probably even help you figure out how to make it happen. On moving day, check to make sure the utilities are working—before nighttime. You don't want to learn your electricity or heat didn't get turned on when it's already dark and cold.

Check to make sure the old utilities were shut off, or at least that you're not being charged past the date you asked for them to

Savor the Move

Let's face it, moving can be hectic, to say the least. In some ways it's a good litmus test for the relationships in your life. If, by the time you've packed up your stuff and moved it to a new place, you and your friends or significant other still like each other, you're probably going to be in it for the long haul. But don't let the stress that comes with getting everything packed and unpacked (and perhaps the aches and pains from moving your things) overshadow the joy of starting a new chapter in your life. Once you're able to remember where you put all of your essentials, take a moment to bask in the fact that you did it! You're out on your own and are well on the way to earning that capital "G" in Grown-up.

be shut off. Most of the time you can double-check your account online to make sure the bill is closed out, but you may want to call to confirm, too.

What Do You Do When the Heat Goes Out in the Middle of the Night?

This has happened to me more times than I can count. Most of the time it hasn't been my fault, but a couple times it was. (For example, I forgot to get oil delivered to the house I bought in my early adult years and it ran out. (If this is something you need to do, considering setting up an arrangement with your oil company for automatic delivery.) When that was the case, I had to bundle up in all my warm clothes and blankets, suck it up until morning, call the oil company, and pay extra for same-day fuel delivery.

But there have been times when the heat went out for reasons not of my own doing. Sometimes it's because the power goes out and you have electric heat. Do a quick scan to see if it looks like the whole neighborhood is out of power. If so, call the electric company to report it. If not, flip your circuit breaker (Google it) to see if it needs to be reset. If that doesn't work, call your landlord, who may want you to notify the electric company. If your electricity is on and your heat is not, call your landlord.

If you own your home and have a furnace (and know there's oil in the tank or the gas is working), check to see if it is running. If not, flip the emergency switch to see if it will kick back on. If it doesn't, I'm sorry to say you're going to have to call someone to fix it. And keep in mind that in many cases, no heat also means no hot water. That's always good to know before you jump in the shower.

Furnishing Your New Home

Look at what you've gotten done by now. You have a place to live, you (maybe) have a roommate to live with, and you have a date to move in. That's a big deal. So, what are you going to bring with you? If it's not your first apartment, the answer probably is: My clothes, my stuff, and the furniture that's mine to take, along with other items that will survive being moved and don't smell awful. If it's your first apartment, the answer probably is: My clothes and stuff. Now you're probably wondering how you'll furnish the place after spending a good chunk of money just to live there. Don't despair. It's amazing what you can come up with when you have friends, family, co-workers, and even just a little money.

You Don't Have to Get Everything at Once

Start with what you need. When it really comes down furniture, that's not a whole lot. Here's what you need to get started:

- A place to sleep
- A place to sit
- Somewhere to store your clothes
- A surface on which to eat and maybe work

So, you're looking at maybe a bed, a couch, a dresser, and some sort of table. If buying all of those things is out of your price range, think about what can serve more than one function. It's a total cliché, but people buy futons for a reason. They function as both a place to sleep and a place to sit. If you managed to find a place with a closet, you may not even need a dresser, just a bunch of hangers and some portable plastic drawers or storage bins. A table can be a surface on which to eat and a place to work. If that's not doable, a couple of decent TV trays will do the trick.

Beggars Sometimes Can Be Choosers

Don't underestimate the generosity of friends and family, but be careful they don't use your asking for any spare furnishings as an opportunity to pawn off things that can't even be donated to charity. When I panic-signed the lease on my apartment post-divorce, I walked into it with absolutely nothing. When my co-workers found out, one of them said, "Why don't you come see what I have in my barn?" (That's New England-speak for not-quite garage and not-quite storage building.) She told me to take what I wanted. I walked away with almost everything I needed, including a bed, kitchen table, dresser, full-length mirror, microwave cart/kitchen storage unit, and the microwave to go with it.

It Doesn't Have to Be Expensive or Fancy

You don't have to go all out unless you plan to rent your apartment to film companies for commercials. You can find good, useable stuff at garage sales, yard sales, flea markets, discount stores, etc. My first kitchen table was a plastic patio table I bought for about $10 with matching plastic chairs that were not at all stylish, sturdy, or even comfortable. But there were four of them, and I could have guests over. It didn't even matter that there was a hole in the middle of the table for a patio umbrella. The pepper mill my grandmother gave me fit perfectly in that spot, and it added a little class. But many places also have non-patio-table options at affordable prices that look great!

8 |
WHEN IN DOUBT, THROW IT OUT

Cooking, Cleaning, and Food Shopping

Adulting involves housework. You think you've finally got the dishes or laundry done, and then they're dirty again. It's enough to make me wish clothes were disposable and I could eat with plastic utensils and paper plates all the time. But of course, it's not just environmentally unsound, it's also not a very grown-up look. Let's start with your kitchen.

Knowing Your Way Around the Kitchen

So let's introduce you to the basics of your kitchen. You'll probably want a microwave for the convenience of easily heating up that cup of coffee that got cold before you could drink it, instant oatmeal packets, frozen foods, etc. Oh, and if you drink coffee, you're going to want some sort of coffee maker.

You also have the stove, which is the top part of the range with the burners. Then there's the oven, the place not just to store your broiler pan and miscellaneous other things, but to actually cook and bake food. Many stoves and ovens are electric, but some are gas. The good thing about a gas stove is that you can control the heat on the burners much more accurately. But if you have an older gas stove (more than about twenty years old), you may need to re-light the pilot light every once in a while. Make sure you have the manual for your stove so you can figure out how to do that if necessary. (There may also be instructions on the door of the oven or underneath the stove top.) If you don't have the manual, ask your landlord for one. Or, you could look up the model online and download the manual.

The oven has a drawer underneath. Most people use it to store pots and pans, but it's really a warming drawer. If you're making more than one dish, you can put the finished one in that drawer to keep it warm while you make the next one. I'm going to be honest—I still just store pots and pans in that drawer.

You have your refrigerator, freezer, and cupboards. When you first move in, they're going to be empty. That's because as an adult, you are expected to buy the food that is stored there. That first trip to grab the basics can be expensive, so brace yourself.

Making the Most of Your Grocery Shopping List

You don't have to buy everything at an expensive grocery store. And you don't have to buy name-brand supplies either. Most basic supplies, like ketchup and flour, can be bought at big-box stores or even dollar stores. Those are the kinds of things that don't need name cachet. The generic or store brand works just as well, and tastes pretty much the same.

If You Smell Gas!

On older gas ranges (more than about twenty years old), it is important to keep the pilot light on. If you don't, gas could leak out, which is not only a huge a fire hazard, but it can also make you sick. This is less likely with more modern ranges, which have more safety features. But if your range is older, make sure you know if the pilot light needs to stay lit. If you ever smell the "rotten egg" odor of escaping gas, turn the gas valve to "off" if you can, immediately leave the place, and call the fire department, the local gas company, and your landlord.

My friend's mother told her to choose one thing that you always want to buy the name brand version of, and then let the rest slide. That's such good advice. For her, it's sneakers. For me, it's laundry detergent. My husband always buys name-brand dish liquid. My kids always want name-brand cereal. I did, too, when I was a kid, but I learned my mother used to buy one box of name-brand cereal and when it was gone, she'd buy the generic and transfer it to the name-brand box (both disappointing and brilliant). Think about what your nonnegotiable is going to be. It will make you feel less like you're depriving yourself.

Basics

(This List Assumes You Plan to Do Some Baking and Cooking)

- All-purpose flour
- Sugar (white and brown—if you make cookies, you're going to need both, good to know, right?)
- Baking powder
- Baking soda
- Salt
- Pepper
- Cinnamon
- Garlic powder or salt
- Cocoa powder
- Breadcrumbs
- Vanilla extract (again, cookies)
- Vegetable or canola oil
- Nonstick cooking spray
- Vinegar
- Honey
- Rice
- Pasta
- Pasta sauce
- Mustard
- Mayonnaise

- Ketchup
- Jelly or jam
- Pickles (I never have pickles when I want them)
- Soy sauce
- Worcestershire sauce
- Hot sauce
- Milk, soy milk, or almond milk
- Eggs
- Butter or margarine
- Shredded cheese (everything is better with cheese, plus it freezes well)
- Bread
- Coffee
- Tea
- Breakfast cereal
- Oatmeal (instant packets for a quick breakfast and/or old-fashioned rolled oats for baking)

Optional Snacks and Meal-Making Items...............

- Crackers
- Dried or canned fruit (such as applesauce)
- Peanut or almond butter
- Chicken broth
- Canned vegetables (beans, corn, tomatoes, olives)
- Canned tuna or chicken
- Fresh produce
- Tofu

- Meat (chicken, ground beef, stew beef, etc.)
- Fish
- Lunch meat
- Bacon
- Nuts
- Ice cream
- Frozen vegetables
- Popcorn
- Drinks

Non-Food Grocery Items ....

- Disinfectant wipes (and/or all-purpose disinfecting cleaning spray)
- Paper towels
- Napkins (optional—you can use cloth napkins or paper towels)
- Aluminum foil
- Sandwich and freezer bags
- Reusable plastic food containers with lids

- Dishwashing liquid or dishwasher detergent
- Sponges
- Dish scrub brush
- Plastic wrap
- Trash bags
- Dish drying rack (if you don't have one)
- Ice-cube trays
- Rubber gloves (you don't want dishpan hands!)

Stocking Your Kitchen: Utensils and Cookware

In my first apartment, I had an interesting collection of mismatched utensils, plates, and cookware. That is, once it occurred to me that I needed these things at all. The very basics you need are plates, bowls, forks, knives, spoons, glasses, and cups. But there are other essentials for your new kitchen, especially if you plan to stick to your budget and not eat out all the time.

10 Cooking Utensils to Have on Hand

1. Cooking knives. A butter knife can only get you so far. If you can only afford one good cooking knife, make it a chef's knife. It can be used to prep food and cut cooked food. You may also want to splurge on a serrated knife (for slicing bread, etc.) so guests don't have to wait to use The Knife. A paring knife for small produce comes in handy, too, if you're going wild.

2. Measuring spoons. Just buy a set. You can grab them at a dollar store, they nest together, and you're not going to be able to gauge ¼ teaspoon without it. Trust me.

3. Measuring cups. If you're planning on baking, get a set for dry ingredients with at least a quarter cup, half cup, and one cup. Also get a one-quart (four cups or thirty-two ounces) measuring cup for liquids. Dry ingredients and liquids are measured differently, though the cups hold the same volume, because they're designed to do a better job of measuring each type of ingredient.

4. Wooden spoons. You can stir with them without making that awful scraping noise or damaging your pans, and you can use two of them to look fancy when you serve salad.

5. Metal or stiff plastic spatula. This is the one that I call the "flippy" spatula. You can scoop under things like cookies or hamburgers, and flip them over easily.

Do the Dishes Regularly

If you're cooking and eating, there are going to be dirty dishes. It's just unavoidable. Some people hate to do the dishes and let them pile up in the sink and on the counter until they run out of space or clean dishes to use. I'm a do-the-dishes-as-you-go kind of person. I wash the bowls, measuring cups, measuring spoons, or other dishes I used while my meal is cooking. My husband is a wait-until-the-last-minute kind of person. He cooks, lets the dishes sit in the sink, and tackles them after the meal along with the plates, cups, etc. Either way, the dishes get done once the meal is over. You don't have to do them immediately, but do wash them at the end of the day (or first thing in the morning if you had to let a pot soak in bubbly water overnight to loosen whatever stuck to the bottom of it). Because here's the thing: Dirty dishes not only ruin the aesthetic of your kitchen, they also start to smell bad and attract ants and other little bugs.

6. Vegetable peeler. You could try to peel potatoes, apples, or carrots with a knife, but it's easier to just have a vegetable peeler. It can also be used to shave cheese or make chocolate curls for garnish. (I know, I know. I'm just saying you can. You don't have to.)

7. Ladle. Here's the thing—you cannot easily serve stews or soups without a ladle. It just doesn't work. And you can hook the ladle to the side of a pot if you get one with a super-handy bent handle.

8. Whisk. A whisk with thin wires can help you mix wet ingredients together and also make sure that sauces don't stick to the bottom of a saucepan.

9. Rubber spatula. This is the "squishy" tool. It's the one you use to scrape the last of the batter into a pan or the rest of the peanut butter out of the jar.

10. Slotted spoon. How else are you going to get the eggshells out of something without using your fingers?

5 Cookware Items to Have on Hand

1. Non-stick frying pan. If you ever make eggs, bacon, pancakes, or stir fry, you're going to need this. You can buy a two-piece set to have a small one and a larger one so you can cook two things at once.

2. A saucepan. A four-quart saucepan is just the right size to cook everything from a can of soup to a pot of pasta.

3. A twelve-quart stock pot. This comes in handy if you're making a lot of soup! Or, you know, boiling lobsters or pasta to go with the sauce you're making in your saucepan.

4. Sheet pans (aka cookie sheets). Kind of self-explanatory, right? Yes, you can make cookies, but you can also heat up frozen foods and cook meat on them.

5. Glass baking dishes. An eight-inch glass baking dish is perfect for casseroles, pot pies, and other one-dish meals. It also fits in a microwave!

7 Other Kitchen Tools to Have on Hand

1. A cutting board. A cutting board not only protects your fingers, it also protects your counters from getting scratched up. I recommend a plastic board that can be both wiped down with bleach and put into a dishwasher for full disinfecting. (Some cutting boards are made with antimicrobial material. Those are the best!)

2. Colander (aka strainer). You'll need this to drain pasta, wash produce, and other things. I'd totally recommend getting one that has feet that let it stand up off the bottom of the sink.

3. Mixing or "prep" bowls. When you cook, you'll need small and large bowls to mix ingredients in. You can either buy a set of mixing bowls or combination mixing bowls/containers of various sizes, often with lids. Attractive ceramic, glass, metal, or even plastic ones can be used as serving dishes, and a set with lids can also store leftovers easily. It's a toss-up, whatever you prefer. If you want to store leftovers in serving dishes without lids, you can also cover the tops with foil or plastic wrap.

4. Can opener. Do yourself a favor and buy yourself a manual can opener, and get good at using it (being careful of sharp edges, though). If the electricity goes out, or the apocalypse comes, you're not going to be able to use an electric one. And you'll be hungry if you can't get into your emergency canned-food stash.

5. Cooling rack. True story: I once made an amazing chicken cordon bleu, took the dish out of the oven, put it on top of the stove, and then quickly ducked as the glass dish exploded from the residual heat. Needless to say, we had pizza that night, and I bought a wire-mesh cooling rack the next day.

6. Oven mitts or potholders. Obviously, these are to protect your hands from the hot oven and hot cookware.

7. Tongs. These are great for dishing up pasta, flipping steaks, and keeping you at arm's length when pan-frying anything.

A Quick Note on Cleaning Out the Fridge

Here's the note: Take some time to clean the refrigerator before it turns on you. In all seriousness, once leftovers start growing mold or unused produce liquefies, it's much harder to clean and reduce odor. Just take half an hour once a week to remove all food from the fridge (this will allow you to clean all the corners and crevices), throw out old leftovers, and clean out less-than-prime foods. Then either wipe down the shelves and drawers with cleaning wipes (you can also use paper towels and cleaning spray), or remove them for washing with water and dish soap.

Again, just remember to remove the food before you wipe the shelves down. It can sit on the counter for a little bit while you get any spills or crumbs that may be underneath or behind your food.

3 Quick, Easy Meals to Impress Your Friends and Family

I remember so clearly the first dinner party I threw. I felt like such an adult and was really proud of myself. My boyfriend at the time had family visiting from out of town, so I decided to make something to impress them. The food was delicious, but not plentiful (because I was poor). Later, it got back to me that the relatives were appalled that there wasn't enough food for seconds. All these years later, that still stings. I don't want you to ever feel like that. Here are some quick-and-easy recipes to try that also tell you how many people they'll serve, so when it's dinner-party time, you'll be ready. You can double them if you need to, and make sure to have salad, vegetables, or other side dishes to fill out the meal.

Chicken Pot Pie (for 4 People)

1 ⅔ cups	frozen mixed vegetables (thawed)
1 cup	cooked, diced chicken (you can buy strips of chicken in deli packages and just cut them into small cubes)
10-ounce	can cream of chicken soup
1 cup	Bisquick baking mix
½ cup	milk
1	egg

Preheat oven to 400°F. Mix vegetables, chicken, and soup in an ungreased eight-inch baking dish (a pie pan or square casserole dish). (Don't add liquid to the soup, keep it condensed. It's going to look a little gross and jiggly, but that's right.) Put the Bisquick in a small bowl, and then add the milk and egg. Mix them together with a fork. Then, pour the batter into the pie pan so that it covers the chicken and vegetable mixture. Bake for thirty minutes or until the top is golden brown.

Chicken Tetrazzini (for 6 People)

½ cup	butter or margarine (this is one stick or 8 tablespoons)
1½ cups	spaghetti
¼ cup	flour
2 cups	milk
1½ tsp	salt
¼ tsp	pepper
1 cup	shredded cheddar cheese (this is half of an 8-ounce package)
1½ cups	cooked, diced chicken (you can buy strips of chicken in deli packages and just cut them into small cubes)
½ cup	mushrooms, sliced (you can use canned ones, just drain all the liquid first)
¾ cup	breadcrumbs

Preheat oven to 325°F. Use a little butter or non-stick cooking spray to grease the bottom and sides of a rectangular casserole dish. Cook the spaghetti according to package directions and set it aside. (I tend to just leave it in the strainer in the kitchen sink.)

Melt half the butter or margarine in a medium-sized saucepan on medium heat. Slowly add the flour and stir with a wooden spoon until it's blended. Turn the heat down to low. Keep stirring, and add the milk a little at a time. Then, add the salt, pepper, and cheese. Stir until the cheese melts and the sauce thickens a little. You may need to turn the heat up a little to get it to thicken.

Add the chicken and mushrooms to the sauce. Then add the spaghetti. Mix it all together. Pour it into the casserole dish. Melt the other half of the butter or margarine and mix the breadcrumbs into it. Sprinkle that mixture on top of the casserole. Bake at 325° for twenty-five minutes.

Parmesan Tilapia (for 4 People)

½ cup   Parmesan cheese (we call this "shaky cheese" in our house; it's the stuff that comes in green cylinders)

¼ cup   butter or margarine left out to soften (this is one stick or 8 tablespoons)

3 tbsp   mayonnaise

½ tsp   pepper

¼ tsp   celery salt (this isn't what it sounds like; it's a spice and you can find it in the baking aisle of the grocery store)

¼ tsp   onion powder

2 lbs   tilapia (the great thing about tilapia is that you can buy fresh or frozen fillets, and it's fairly inexpensive, but if you buy the frozen fillets, just make sure to defrost them before making this recipe)

Preheat the broiler of your oven. On some ovens, there's one setting that says "broil," while on others, there are two broil settings—in this case, use high. Then, line the broiler pan with tin foil. (That's the pan that usually comes with the oven. It has a slotted cookie-sheet-like cover that sits on top of the pan. You put the tin foil between the slotted cover and the bottom half of the pan.) Spray cooking spray on the slotted top.

Mix the "shaky" cheese, butter, and mayonnaise together in a small bowl. Add the pepper, celery salt, and onion powder. Mix again and set the bowl aside.

Put the tilapia fillets on the top of the broiler pan. Put them in the oven and broil them just a few inches from the top heating element of the oven for three minutes. Take the pan out (using an oven mitt or potholder!) and use a spatula to flip the fillets over. Smooth the mayo mixture on the top of each fillet. Put them back in to broil for three minutes or until the topping is slightly browned and the fish flakes when you put a fork in it.

Getting the Bathroom in Order

The bathroom is likely to be the smallest room in your place, but it's arguably the most important. Aside from the obvious reasons, it's where you'll shower, groom, and it's the one room in your place to which you can't really deny visitors entry.

When you move in, bring toilet paper with you. It's not likely to be there waiting for you, and it's a necessity. And while you're at it, make sure you have hand soap for washing your hands after you use the bathroom.

Unless you move into a place with a shower that has glass doors, be sure you have a shower rod. Not all places come with one. If yours doesn't, measure the top of the shower side-to-side, and buy a rod that fits, along with a shower curtain, hooks to go with it, and a plastic liner. You're going to want the plastic liner so your shower curtain doesn't get soaked. Or if you're strapped for cash, just get the shower liner. The liner should go inside the tub when you shower, to keep the water from going out on to the floor. Also make sure you have a bathmat or towel to put on the floor in front of the shower so you don't slip, slide, and hurt yourself when you get out of the shower. I'm a bit of a klutz, so I'd also buy the adhesive safety mat for the inside of the tub, too. But that's just me. You're welcome to live on the wilder side.

Essential Bathroom Supplies

Some of them are obvious, while others aren't. Here's a beginner's list of bathroom supplies, starting with personal items:

- Toilet paper (it's worth noting again)
- Body wash or soap
- Shampoo and conditioner
- Toothbrush and toothpaste
- Mouthwash
- Dental floss
- Razors
- Shaving cream
- Bath towels
- Hand towels
- Toilet brush, cleansers, plunger, bucket

How Do You Unclog the Toilet?

Ideally, you have in your bathroom a plunger available to quickly unclog the toilet. If you do, don't forget to put down newspapers or old towels around the toilet to seep up any overflow. But if you don't have a plunger on hand, you can try a couple of other tricks:

- Put about a quarter cup of liquid dish soap in the toilet bowl and let it sit for about ten minutes. Then pour in a pot of hot (not boiling) water and let it sit again. The combination of the two may loosen and lubricate the clog enough for it to begin to drain.

- Use a wire hanger as a makeshift plumbing snake. Untwist it, leaving the hook on the end, throw on some plastic gloves, and push the hook end of the hanger into the toilet drain to snag or break up the clog.

- Bail out some of the extra water from your toilet (if it's not just nasty beyond belief) and then try creating a third-grade-science-fair volcano in your toilet bowl. Pour equal parts vinegar and baking soda into the toilet, watch it bubble and boil, wait half an hour, and then pour a cup of hot water after it.

Cleaning the Bathroom

Have a plunger on hand and a plastic bucket to keep it in. That's a full stop nonnegotiable (but see the previous page if you don't have one yet). Don't buy the bell-shaped plunger you see character actors carrying on their shoulders in movies. They don't work well for toilet emergencies. Instead, buy a beehive plunger or a bellows plunger. A beehive plunger is a rounded cylinder that's wider in the middle and narrows to a lip at the bottom. It fits into the drain of the toilet to make a complete seal (this is very important). A bellows plunger looks like an accordion. As you plunge, the ridges collapse and expand so you can create a pressure seal. It will also help you avoid spillage when you plunge.

Moving on, because we really don't need to dwell on that sh*t. You're also going to need cleansers for your bathroom. Have a toilet brush on hand and foaming toilet cleanser. Just spray it around the inside of the toilet bowl (including up under the rim), and then use the brush to scrub the inside of the toilet.

You may want disposable gloves for the rest of the cleaning. You can use bathroom cleaning spray along with rags, paper towels, or a sponge to wipe down the sink, the back of the toilet, and your bathtub.

If you have tile shower walls, they should be cleaned with tile cleaner to keep soap scum from building up. If you have an acrylic tub surround, use a nonabrasive cleaner for bathrooms. And you're likely to need to use drain cleaner for the sink and the shower drain at some point. As soon as you notice that the drain is slowing down, grab a bottle of drain cleaner, read the directions very carefully, and use it. The important thing to remember is that it usually needs to sit for at least an hour and be rinsed down with cold water. Hot water will create steam that combines with the cleaner to make caustic fumes. And you don't want to get any drain cleaner on your skin, or breathe in any fumes.

GETTING THE REST OF THE HOUSE IN ORDER

You're probably exhausted by now. That's OK. You can take a break, but know there's more to keeping your home in order, too. Some people might tell you to make your bed every morning, but I'm not one of them. I will, however, tell you to change or wash your sheets weekly or biweekly.

10 Steps for Doing Laundry

If you're lucky enough to have a washer-dryer or laundry room where you live, it's easier to keep on top of doing the laundry. You can do a couple of small loads a week. If you have to go to a laundromat, you'll probably need  to dedicate some time to get there and wash and dry your clothes. Bring a book, find a laundromat with Wi-Fi, or find a laundromat-coffee-shop combo so you can socialize while you're living your best adult life. If you've never done laundry, I've got you covered. I like to vacuum, but I also like doing laundry. It's satisfying. But I also don't have to go to a laundromat anymore. Anyway…here's how to do your laundry. At the very least, you're going to need a good, general-purpose laundry detergent.

1 | Read labels.

The labels on your clothes, towels, and sheets will say whether or not they can be machine washed. They'll also tell you if something has to be washed in a certain temperature of water or on a specific type of cycle. Pay attention. The last thing you want to do is end up with shrunken clothes that are dyed pink from the one red towel that needed to be washed separately.

2 | Sort your clothes.

Set aside anything that says, "wash separately," "hand wash," or "dry clean only." Then promptly throw it away and never wear it again because that's too much upkeep. (I'm kidding! Kind of.)

Then sort by color. Put all whites in one pile. Put all light grays and light colors in one pile. Put all dark-colored clothes (black, dark blue, brown, dark gray) together. Lastly, put all bright colors together (especially reds, which should have their own load). Those are all separate loads. Be sure to check pockets for stray items and turn inside out any items that have fancy flair, like sequins or beads.

3 | Pretreat stains.

Put stain remover or a bit of laundry detergent on any prominent stains. I usually have at least two shirts that have coffee stains on them.

4 | Read the detergent directions on the bottle or box.

You need to figure out how much detergent to use for the size of the laundry load. Some detergents are concentrated, which means you don't have to use as much. Determine how much to use based on the size of the load by reading the label. Add the laundry soap to the washing machine before you put the clothes in so it doesn't leave detergent deposits on your clothes.

5 | Pick a water temperature.

Most laundry can be washed in cold water, which saves you any unexpected shrinking. That said, cotton underwear, sheets, face masks, and anything else you have the germ heebie-jeebies about should be washed in hot water to sanitize them.

6 | Pick the cycle.

Most of the time the normal cycle is best, but if things are really dirty, you may want to use heavy duty. Also, if you're washing what my mother used to call your "unmentionables," you'll want to use the delicate cycle, especially if your unmentionables are lacy or made of silk. This is also the cycle to use for those items with fancy flair, like sequins or beads.

7 | Load the washer.

Try not to just dump everything in at once. It can make the wash load unbalanced and some clothes may not get clean. Load the washer evenly, so that the laundry is balanced inside. Doing this a little more thoughtfully also gives you a second chance to check pockets for stray items, as well as to make sure all laundry is with its proper load. (Again, you don't want a stray red sock turning all your whites pink.)

8 | Unload the machine ASAP after the cycle ends.

There's nothing worse than forgetting to remove a load, leaving it overnight, and then trying to figure out what smells musty. (It's the laundry. You'll have to redo the load.) Avoid that by taking things out as soon as possible and putting them in the dryer or hanging them to dry.

9 | Decide what to hang dry.

Drying certain items in a dryer can shrink them. Look at the label, and if it says "tumble dry," it's fine. Otherwise, it's not. Ten years ago, my husband shrunk my favorite nightgown. I've yet to forgive him. And now he hangs up almost all of my clothes to dry when he does laundry. It's a bit of an overreaction, but I appreciate the thought. If it can't afford to shrink, don't put it in the dryer.

10 | Load the dryer.

Put all heavier clothes in the dryer at once (like jeans and towels), and then dry lighter-weight items as a separate load. It allows you to use the right temperature setting and makes it less likely that you'll shrink clothes or have to run the dryer again. Don't overcrowd the dryer, though, because that will slow things down.

A Last Look: Managing Clutter and Dust

A lot of keeping your home in order is about staying organized. If you have a place for everything and you put it all where it belongs, it's much easier to maintain.

Take the time to buy hangers and hooks to hang up clothes and towels. Buy a laundry hamper or basket, too, and put dirty clothes in it instead of leaving them on your bedroom floor. Invest in some under-the-bed boxes to store out-of-season clothes out of

sight. If you can afford it, invest in a vacuum cleaner. If you can't (which would be reasonable because a good vacuum cleaner is not inexpensive), figure out which one of your nearby friends, neighbors, or family members has one they'll let you borrow at least once a month.

Grab some bookshelves or crates to store books. Have a place for bills to be paid, even if it's a shoebox. Throw away junk mail, food wrappers, Amazon packaging, and other trash so it's not sitting around. Look around your rooms, and tidy up the stray throw pillows, blankets, charger cords you're not using, birthday cards from two months ago, and so on. Run some dusting or disinfecting wipes over the furniture, window sills, baseboard heat covers, lamps, pictures, and electronics every week or two. Vacuum the floor and any upholstered furniture (especially if you have any pets that like to hang out there) every week or so, too. A little organization and a few minutes of effort go a long way.

9 |
GETTING
PLACES
Planes, Trains, Automobiles, and More

Traveling to places you've never been before can be daunting, but it's also exciting! I love being places, but I have the worst sense of direction in the world and a bit of claustrophobia, neither of which serves me well when I have to take trains, planes, buses, or frankly, walk from one place to another.

I'm the person you see standing on the street corner with my phone in my hand turning in circles to try to figure out how to read which end of the arrow I am on Google Maps. When my New York City colleagues tell me I just have to go uptown a few blocks, I look at them panic-stricken. And yet (at least when we're not in the midst of a pandemic), I travel often for work and to places I've never been before, which is fun, and also builds a sense of self-confidence. And you can do it, too!

Navigating Public Transportation

Sometimes I have to deal with being lost and nervous more often than I ought to admit while navigating public transportation systems, whether I want to or not. After all, it is the best and most inexpensive way to get from point A to point B. Taxis and Uber or Lyft fees add up really quickly and aren't practical if you're on a budget. And they're really impractical if you don't have a car, and you're trying to get from point A to point B in the city or town you live in.

Most cities have transit cards that you can add money to if you're going to be using the trains and buses regularly. Many of them offer student discounts and discounts for monthly cards. In fact, a number of employers in big cities may offer transit cards as part of their benefits program.

Despite my anxiety about public transport, I have an MTA card for Boston, a Metro card for New York, a Breeze Card for Atlanta, and a Ventra Card for Chicago in my wallet. They don't expire right away, so I hold on to them just in case. You may not need all of those cards in your wallet, but there is some information you need to know in order to navigate public transportation confidently.

Know the Hours and Timing

Know when buses and trains start and stop running. Look it up on the transit's website. It's especially important to know what your options are late at night and on weekends. Most cities have a pretty predictable set schedule, which, unpredictably, changes late at night and on weekends, when they run less frequently. It's good to know that before you get stranded somewhere unfamiliar.

It's also good to know about how long it will take you to get from your home or office to the bus stop or train station. It's a miraculous transit system that runs on time, and you're going to want to make sure to be there early in case the bus or train isn't running on time, or it's going to be so crowded that you may have to take the next one. Or, it could be running early (ha!) and you don't want it to leave without you.

Make Sure You've Got the Right Route

I may not have a good sense of direction, but I always know the route number and end destination of the line of transportation I take. Keep in mind the end destination is not always going to be the same as your stop, so knowing the end destination allows you to check the digital crawl on the side or front to confirm you've got the right one. Read that digital crawl. And if you're not totally sure the bus is going to stop for you, take the chance on waving the driver down, hitting the button, or pulling the cord (whichever is available). You might feel silly, but at least you'll make it on time to where you're going.

Have Correct Change or Your Pass Ready to Go

Transit systems may not always run on time, but they try hard. That means they're moving people on and off buses and trains quickly. Most buses ask you to have the exact change on hand if you're going to pay cash, so don't expect to get change back if you don't. And if you're using a pass, have it ready to swipe or hand to the conductor as they come through the train car. If your pass is on your smartphone, have it up and ready to scan.

Remember Hand Sanitizer!

This is self-explanatory, but where there are a lot of people or a place where a lot of people pass through, there are also lot of viruses and germs. I always carry hand sanitizer with me because I can't always find a place to wash my hands after I get off a plane, train, or bus. If you can, try to get a small bottle that you can hook to the outside of the bag you carry. That way you don't have to shuffle through the rest of your things before you sanitize—it's accessible and ready to use.

Mind Your Manners

Manners have taken a backseat over time. People are busy, they want to get where they're going, and often other people are in their way. It's really easy to get caught up in the crowd mentality of needing to get on the plane or train RIGHT now. But, it's actually easier to at least wait for some of the passengers who need to get off to do so before you push your way past them. Then you can push and shove all you want. (I'm kidding!)

And if the bus or train is crowded, think twice before you give the seat next to you over to your bag instead of another human. I will say this, though: Don't ever feel like you have to apologize if your body takes up more room than other people expect it to or that you need to prove you have a disability that requires you to ask for the seat the law allows you.

This is a lesson I wished I'd learned earlier in my adult life. People come in all shapes, sizes, and health statuses, and they all need to get places. If someone is upset that you're taking up "too much space," that's not on you. You also don't owe anyone proof of your disability. And, if you can, offer to give up your seat for the elderly, expectant mothers, or people holding babies or toddlers.

Make the Most of Your Smartphone

The days of foldout maps that never quite fold back up correctly are fast fading. I mean, you can grab paper maps of transit routes, but most cities have apps that are fairly easy to use. Google Maps and apps like Embark work just as well, too. That is, if you're not going to walk in circles while you look at it like I do.

How to Read the Map

If you're looking at a transit map for the first time, I'm not going to lie. It can be overwhelming. What are all those colored lines and dots and letters and times? The simple answer is that the colored lines and letters show the different routes. The dots are the different stops along the way. And the times tend to show when the bus or train is supposed to be at the location. The nice thing about transit apps is they often are updated in real time, so you know when a bus or train is running late.

Some maps in transit apps have static timetables, though. They show the times when the train or bus gets to and leaves from each stop. The timetables are usually colored-coded to match the route. That way if you know you're taking the green line, you can scroll down to the green-highlighted route.

Where it gets tricky and makes me wish I could afford to take taxis all the time is when it comes to transferring. Sometime there's not a direct route to where you're going.

Look on the map for a route that has a stop where you're starting out. Then, find the route that goes to your end destination. Most of the time, they have a common stop. That's where you're going first. You'll need to time it well, though, and make sure you get to that stop with enough time to change buses or trains. Factor in the need to cross platforms or the street.

Buying a Car

Here's the deal: You may need to buy a car if you decide that public transportation isn't for you or if you live somewhere that doesn't have a robust transit system. (Maine, I'm looking at you.)

Buying a car is a Very Adult Move, and there a are few things to keep in mind. The first is that you're likely to get a better deal if you have some money to put down. The second is that you may have to settle for a used car you can afford instead of a brand new one you love, but for which you can't afford the payments. The third is that a car is an ongoing cost.

You'll have to factor in the cost of gas, maintenance, and, of course, car insurance, which is more expensive before you turn twenty-five years old. I mean, I know for a fact that research shows brain development, especially around impulse control, isn't fully complete until you're around twenty-five, but I didn't know that car insurance companies read the same research I do. If you're in the market to buy a car, here are some good steps to take along the way.

1 | Set a realistic budget.

If you can buy a decent used car from a friend or someone you trust for a few thousand dollars and can afford it, you're in good shape. Otherwise, I'm just going to assume you're going to have to make payments. Figure out what you can afford to pay per month, and remember to factor in the cost of gas and insurance, not just your car payment. This means going all the way back and revisiting your budget.

2 | Think through your transportation needs.

What do you need your vehicle to do? Is it enough for you to fit into the car and just be able to drive it to and from places? Or, do you need to be able to fit all of your friends or lots of stuff in the vehicle, too? That's the difference between looking at a mid-size sedan or an SUV or minivan. Of course, your taste in vehicles matters, too, but if you love a two-seater convertible, you're not going to be able to play the role of designated driver for your entire friend group.

3 | Know what you want vs. what you need.

This is a familiar refrain. It's about thinking through what you can't go without (like a roof rack if you camp, ski, or bike) versus what might be nice to have (like a sun roof). If you're going to be miserable without air conditioning, get it. If you don't care about lane departure technology, don't pay extra for it. But do make sure you have all of your needs and a few of your wants. Your first car doesn't have to be the best car in the world, but it should at least make you happy to drive it.

4 | Do some research (like, for real).

Again, the internet is amazing. There's a ton of information out there on really reputable websites, like Kelly Blue Book (kbb.com), about cars, their safety records, their gas mileage, and all the other things you may want to know. Use that amazing internet to learn something about the cars you can afford before you wander on to a car lot. You can also ask people you know who have cars what they do or don't like about the car they have.

5 | Find a reputable car dealer.

Ask around and see what types of experiences people have had at various dealerships. Walk onto the lot and see what kind of vibe you get. And think about staying away from dealerships where most of the sales staff aren't with other customers. I mean, where are all the customers? And if you feel pressured by the sales staff, it's OK to walk away and go to another dealership.

6 | Take a test drive.

You may love the look of a car, be able to manage the price, and know it has good reviews. But do you like driving it? Take it for a test drive. It's an important move. You need to know whether you can comfortably reach the pedals, adjust the mirrors, lean your seat back, manage the blind spots, figure out how to use all the controls, and more. Does it accelerate well? Stop too abruptly? Idle OK at stoplights? Drive it for thirty minutes to find out, even if you need to take the car salesperson with you.

7 | Know your financing options.

Most dealerships have relationships with banks or have financing, but getting it sorted out and approved is variable depending on your credit history. In some cases, it's a great deal. But in others, you may be offered a high interest rate, asked to put more money down, asked to settle for a shorter-term loan, or asked to pay a higher payment than what you can easily afford. If you don't want to be in a situation where you feel like the dealership has all the power, think about talking to your own bank or even look into a peer-to-peer lending company to get pre-approved financing. This is also one of those times when taking a parent or more-experienced friend with you for help and advice can really pay off.

6 Questions to Ask a Car Salesperson

Buying a car for the first time can be stressful, especially if you've ever heard any jokes about car salesmen. (There don't seem to be as many jokes that use the more gender-neutral term.) It's reasonable to worry about whether you can hold your own. You can. You just need to be prepared. Here are some questions to ask and why they matter.

Can I Take a Test Drive?

You already know why the test drive is important. A car dealer or owner who wants to make a sale and is confident in the condition of the car should readily agree to a test drive. If they say no, walk away.

Do You Have Any Demos for Sale?

If you are looking for a new car, don't think you can afford it, but don't want to buy a much older used car, this is a good in-between option. Demo cars are the new ones dealerships use for test drives or to display in the showroom. Most dealers end up selling demos, and while they only have a few hundred miles on them, that's enough to ask for depreciation costs to be taken off the price.

Where Did This Used Vehicle Come From?

Many used cars come from trade-ins, are demos, are bought at dealer auctions, are previously leased cars, or are maybe even former rental cars. Knowing where it came from helps you get a better sense of whether it has an up-to-date and accurate maintenance history available. It also tells you whether the car has been driven by a ton of people or just a few.

Will You Provide a CARFAX Report?

CARFAX is a third-party vendor that provides a vehicle history report based on the vehicle identification number (VIN). It will tell you maintenance history as well as things like whether the car has ever been in an accident. A reputable dealer has nothing to hide and should be willing to supply that report to you.

What Service Has Been Done on This (Used) Vehicle?

Depending on where a used car came from, it may have been around a while and not in stellar shape when it came onto the lot. If you're considering a used car, especially if it was a former lease, trade-in, or part of a rental fleet, ask what work has been done by the dealer's mechanics and how recently. Then, ask if any service has been planned for the future. It's very possible that you walked onto the lot and fell in love with the car that was going to have its tires rotated or replaced tomorrow. It's better to have it done still so you don't end up paying for that work once you own the car.

Will You Take My Old Car as a Trade-in?

This is a great question if you're replacing your old car (emphasis on old). Even if you're not going to get a lot of financial value for your trade-in, it means you don't have to find a buyer or another way to get rid of your car.

OWNING A CAR

Hooray, you're a car owner! You can hit the open road. And make sure you have it registered and insured, check your tire pressure once a month, keep your windshield wiper fluid filled, and get the oil changed on time. For many cars, you need to change the oil every three months or 3000 miles, whichever comes first, but others can go longer these days. I'm not good about remembering, so I'm glad that the oil change place puts a sticker on my windshield telling me the date or mileage I should be looking for.

Pumping Your Own Gas

Unless you live in a state where someone else pumps the gas for you, you also have the pleasure of learning how to pump gas so you can keep moving while you're on the open road. Or, you know, get to work. But if you've never had a car before, you may not know how to pump gas. Don't worry, I've got you covered.

1 | Park with the fill cover facing the pump.
Don't know which side of the car your fill cover is on? I was about

two years younger than I am now when I learned the arrow next to the gas gauge on your dashboard points to the side the fill cover is on. How easy is that? Now that you know that, the next step is to park about two feet between your car and the pump. Far enough away so you can fit between them and close enough that the hose and nozzle will reach.

2 | Turn off the engine!

Don't skip this step. Just don't. It's a safety issue. It's unlikely to start a fire, but how about you just don't take the chance? Another unusual safety tip: Don't get back in the car while you're pumping gas, don't shut the door or sit down while the gas is still pumping. Opening and shutting the door may release static electricity, and you don't want that to happen near gas or gas fumes. That's why you see so many people half sitting in the driver's seat while they're pumping gas. Just turn off the car, get out, and stand outside while you're pumping the gas.

3 | Pay for and choose your type of gas.

There are a couple of ways you can do this:

- If you're paying cash, you'll probably have to go into the gas station to prepay. Make sure you know the number of the pump your car is at or can at least point to it. They'll set the pump to stop at the amount you prepaid.
- If you're using a debit or credit card, you can usually pay at the pump. Follow the directions on the pump for how to swipe or insert your card. You can then either choose the amount to prepay or just fill the tank and let it charge that whole amount.

There are three types of non-diesel gas you can use: regular, midgrade, and premium. They're priced according to their names. Typically, regular works just fine.

4 | Open the fill cover and insert the nozzle.

There's often a button or lever on the floor next to your driver's seat to pop the fill cover, or else you can just open it from the outside. Once you've done that, unscrew the gas cap. Luckily, in most cars, the cap is attached so you won't put it down and forget to put it back on when you're done. Take the nozzle from the gas pump and place it in your gas tank. You'll know it's right if you let go and the nozzle stays in place.

5 | Pull the trigger.

You don't really pull the "trigger" of the gas nozzle, you squeeze it. You can either just hold it down or use the latch to lock it into place so you don't have to. The pump will be running numbers—it's showing you the amount of money that's adding up as well as how much gas you've pumped. Once the tank is full or it reaches the preset amount you've spent, the nozzle will click off.

6 | Put everything back in order.

Step back a little bit before you take the nozzle out of the gas tank. Otherwise, you might have the pleasure of having some gas drip on you, and you'll smell like it all day. Return the nozzle to the pump, screw the gas cap back on your gas tank, shut the fill cover, grab your receipt, and you're good to go!

What to Do If You're in an Accident

I'm going to tell you the same thing I told both my adult children when they first started driving—I trust you to drive safely; it's the people around you I don't trust. The difference is, I mean it when I say it to you. I haven't seen you drive, so it's easier to believe.

The truth is, you're bound to have at least a little fender bender sometime in your driving career. And the first time it happens, you're going to be so rattled, you won't know what to do. Many insurance companies give you a handy-dandy checklist to keep in the glove compartment, but it's good to know ahead of time, too. In the case of an accident, remember the following:

Safety Comes First

Nothing is more important than making sure you and everyone else has the care they need. Call 911 and let them know you need an ambulance if there are obvious injuries. If not, let them know you need the police for an accident. If you're hurt, and your car is in a safe spot—not in danger of sliding off the road or catching on fire—try to stay in your car until help arrives.

Keep Calm and Carry On

Regardless of whether the damage is done to people or cars, everyone's adrenaline is going to be running super high. Scared people often act mad. And mad people often act mad, too. Keep as calm as you can. Don't engage in an argument with the other driver. If they're really angry and you don't feel safe, stay in your car with the doors locked until the police arrive.

Exchange Information with the Other People Involved

Once you're confident you feel safe, which may be once the police arrive, exchange information with the other driver. If you don't have a pen and paper, you can use a note-taking app and/or camera on your phone. You're going to need to get:

- Names, addresses, and phone numbers of drivers, passengers, and any witnesses. If they won't give it to you, make sure the police have the information for their report.
- The make, models, and license plate numbers of all the vehicles involved. (Make sure to note which state the plate is from, too.)
- The other driver's insurance company, policy numbers, and driver's license numbers.
- Names and badge numbers of the police officers and the number of the accident report. Even if no one is hurt, file an accident report. You'll need it to for any insurance claims.

Document Any Damage

If you're not injured and it's safe to take photos of the damage caused by the accident, do so. Be respectful of the other driver, and make sure you're not taking pictures of any injured passengers or other personal images. Take pictures of all the cars involved, with a particular focus on your own.

Call Your Insurance Company

This can wait until you're home and feel calmer, but you should do it as soon as you can. Let them know what happened and they'll walk you through the process of getting the rest of the information.

Navigating Airlines and Airports

You may have traveled by air before because it's not something only adults do. But you may not have had to navigate buying your own tickets or getting through security without prompting before. If you've got this handled, feel free to skip this section, but you may want to read it just in case there's something you didn't know.

For example, did you know that it's not always cheaper to buy tickets on a third-party travel website? Or that when you do, you're subject to their rules around refunding fares or changing flights? Even if you get a really helpful, sympathetic airline agent on the phone, if you didn't buy your ticket through the airline, they may not be able to change your flight or help you if you went through a third-party website.

Getting the Best Deal on Tickets

Sometimes it's worth it to use a third-party website, like Expedia or Travelocity. You can often book an entire trip, from airfare to hotel to rental car all at once, and there are discounts involved if you do it that way. And if you're not completely and totally loyal to one airline, you can also mix and match outbound and return flights among airlines and even airports to get the best deal. For instance, when I have to go to New York for work, I often fly into one of the three major airports and out of another because of the timing of flights and traffic patterns to and from the city on certain days.

It's worth checking those fares against the price you get directly through the airline's website. They're often the same, if not a little cheaper to buy directly through the airline. Just know that the fare can change even as you are in the process of searching for the flights you want. Make sure to refresh your browser one last time before you purchase to make sure you're seeing the up-to-date price so you don't have to search all over again.

Getting the best deal on tickets isn't just about knowing where to buy them. It's also about knowing what you're willing to compromise to save a little money. You can usually get a less-expensive fare if you don't mind traveling really early in the morning or really late at night.

The fare also varies depending on what's included and if you're flying economy, economy plus, economy premium, or first class. Keep in mind, too, that on some routes, especially those that fly commuter routes with small planes, there's no difference between economy and first class except a curtain. Make sure you're actually getting more space if you're paying for it.

Know What's Included in the Fare

It seems reasonable that when you buy an airline ticket, you should expect it includes some basic things. But, that's apparently not a reasonable expectation anymore. I don't know how often I've gone to purchase a ticket that seems like a really good deal only to be bombarded with an extra fee for every amenity before I finish the transaction. Here are some things you might have to pay extra for:

- **Your luggage.** With most low-cost airlines the base fare means you have a seat on the flight and you can bring a personal item, like a purse, briefcase, or backpack to store under the seat in front of you. It doesn't always automatically include a carry-on bag without extra cost, let alone checking a bag without a fee. Make sure you know whether or not you're going to have to pay an extra fee for the privilege of bringing a duffle bag or rolling carry-on bag with you. If you are going to have to pay an extra fee, see if the cost is comparable to buying the next category of ticket, which is likely to include that carry-on, plus a couple of other amenities. And don't forget to confirm that the fee you'll have to pay for your carry-on bag doesn't increase if you decide to add it on after you've purchased your ticket. Some airlines actually increase that cost if you wait to pay for it on the day of check-in.

- **Your seat.** Not all airlines include in the cost of your ticket the privilege of picking your seat. You'd think that's a given, but it's not. You may not only have to pay more for extra legroom, but also just to choose your seat instead of having it assigned at the gate the day of your flight. If you don't mind where you sit or who you sit with and just want to get where you're going, don't worry about paying the extra fee.

- **Cancellation or change fees.** If you need the flexibility to change your flight or cancel it and get the money back, you're going to have to pay more up front. I have actually been in circumstances where it has been cheaper for me to pay for an entirely new ticket than to pay the $200 change fee. Some airlines will let you make changes and only pay the difference in the fare, but that is becoming harder to find.

- **Booking fees.** I'm just going to say that it's bananas to me that I have to pay extra for the privilege to wait almost an hour on hold to talk to a person who can help me book a flight. But that's more common than not. It's free to book online, but it can cost up to $25 per ticket to book over the phone. If, perchance, you're in a situation where you're trying to change your reservation online and the system won't let you, make sure you tell that to the person on the phone so that you can then ask them to waive any phone-related booking fees.

- **Wi-Fi.** I love flying JetBlue in part because they have free Wi-Fi on their flights. That's not the case for the majority of airlines. It's an amenity you have to pay for. You can pay per hour, per flight or, if you fly a lot, you can buy a monthly subscription plan. That said, I also love being on a short(ish) flight for which I refuse to pay for Wi-Fi because then I can tell people at work that I didn't have Wi-Fi access on the plane in order to answer emails from the air.

What Can I Bring through Security?

You can't bring your soda or full water bottle through security, but the good news is you can bring most snacks, as long as they're not liquid or gel (sorry, Jell-O). That may not sound like good news, but have you seen how much food costs in airports? Other than that, you have to follow the "3-1-1 rule."

That means you can bring liquids and gels, like shampoo, toothpaste, and hand sanitizer, in bottles of up to 3.4 ounces, in one 1-quart bag, and only one bag per passenger. You can also bring your manicure kit, but not your lighter. If you're unsure if you can bring something with you, the good news is that there's a MyTSA app you can download, or you can check the TSA "What Can I Bring?" page on their website.

Get Through Security Faster

1 | Have your ID and boarding pass ready.

Before you get into the security line, pull up your e-boarding pass on your phone and have your ID in the same hand as your phone or tuck the paper pass into your passport.

2 | Dress simply.

Wear shoes you can slip off and on easily and pants that won't slip when you take off your belt. Avoid clothing with metallic threads, or lots of pockets and cuffs. They'll likely show up on the scanner as "suspicious" and you may be pulled aside for a pat down.

3 | Compartmentalize.

You're going to have to take out any electronics bigger than a cell phone and it's likely you may also have to take out food to put it through the scanner. Put all your electronics in one compartment of your carry-on so they can be easily accessed. As to food, consider putting all of your food in one gallon size ziplock bag to set in the security bin.

4 | Scope out who's in the lines.

A shorter line doesn't mean a faster line. Lines with experienced travelers who have their stuff ready to go are likely to move faster than the line that has the family with young children in strollers or a high school sports team.

What If I Miss My Flight?

A friend told me a story about when her daughter was a brand-new adult and she took a trip overseas. The daughter was completely sure she had everything handled. She'd packed, purchased her flights, planned her stays at youth hostels, and even managed the currency exchange on her own. She had a fantastic trip and it was over before she knew it. She headed to the airport at a fairly leisurely pace, confident that she'd make her flight, and even if she didn't it was no big deal. Well, she missed her flight. And it was a big deal.

What she didn't realize was that she couldn't just hop on the next flight. She thought flights were like taxis, if you miss one, you can always just grab the next one. But flights are not like taxis. If you miss one, it can be an ordeal to get on another one, especially if the reason you missed the flight is not the fault of the airline.

If you miss your flight because you didn't get in from a connecting flight in time, the airline is usually happy to work with you to get on another flight or help you get rerouted to your destination. The same is true if you can't get on a flight because of weather-related or mechanical issues. That's because you're already at the airport, you've done your part, and the rest of it is out of your control. In fact, most of it (other than weather) is in the airlines' control.

If you have a legitimate reason for missing the flight and you get there within two hours of when the initial flight departed, you still have reason to hope. A legit reason is pretty confirmable like, "There was a crash on the highway and I was stuck in backed-up traffic for hours." In that case, you may benefit from what's casually referred to as the "flat tire" rule. It's nothing official, but most airlines extend the courtesy and they'll put you on standby for the next available flight. They're much more likely to do so if you call customer service as soon as you know you're not going to make your flight.

On the other hand, if you miss your flight because you didn't get there on time, you got the day or time wrong, or just "weren't feeling it," the airline isn't under any obligation to catch you the next air taxi. Depending on the fare you purchased, they're well within their rights to expect you to pay for a new ticket. You've probably been marked as a no-show and they don't have to return your money, let alone extend you the courtesy of applying it to a new ticket.

Oh, You're Going to Go Places

I may be a hopeless case when it comes to finding my way around without an incipient panic attack, but I have faith you're going to get this—and maybe even love it. When I brought my recently-turned-adult son to visit a college just outside of New York City, he figured out the Long Island Rail Road (LIRR) system in like half an hour, mapped out a route into Manhattan, hopped the train, found his way to the subway and his end destination in no time. And he managed to do all of that in the same amount of time it took me to find my way back to our hotel from the train station.

All that is to say, you've got this. You're flexible, you're adaptable, and damnit, you're an adult. You're not only going to get places; you're also going places!

My best advice other than the obvious "try not to miss your flight," is to be kind, be earnest, and be humble. It's amazing how far a little kindness (with a tinge of panic) can get you when you're asking someone to help you find your way back home again.

Wait, Where's My Luggage?

Sometimes it's not you that misses your flight, it's your luggage. Or, your luggage takes another flight by mistake and you only realize it when you're standing at the baggage carousel watching that one unclaimed bag go 'round and 'round while yours never appears.

Don't panic. Yes, you packed carefully and it seems that your favorite clothes have gone missing, but the good news is the research shows the majority of missing bags aren't lost, they're simply delayed. That means your bag didn't get on the flight in time, but it's likely on the next one.

Talk to your airline's baggage claim office ASAP. If you don't see it, ask at the nearest information desk. Once you're there, let the baggage claim office know your bag didn't show up so you can file a lost bag report. You'll need your boarding pass and the claim ticket for your bag if you have it. (Sometimes it's connected to your boarding pass.) Filing a report triggers the airline to search for your bag. It also lets them know how to reach you when they find it; and, in the off chance it never gets found, that report is what you need to get reimbursed for all the cool clothes and stuff you lost. Make sure to ask for a copy of the report, the name of the person who took it, and the number you can call to get updates on your lost luggage.

10 |
ARGH!
What to Do
When Things
Go Wrong

As much as you plan, prepare, and organize your life, sometimes things go wrong. It's not like they never went wrong before—it's just that before you were in full-on adult mode, there was a grown-up to step in and help fix things. Now, you're that adult.

I remember the first time that realization hit me. My car broke down in the pouring rain in the middle of a busy road while I was on my way to work. As I stood getting soaked by the rain, watching other drivers pass me without stopping while I tried to push my car to the side of the road to get it out of traffic, I thought, "I guess I have to figure this out on my own. Wow."

Things can go wrong in small ways, like locking yourself out of your home or oversleeping, or they can go wrong in big ways, like not being able to pay your rent or having to deal with natural disasters.

Redefining "What Can Go Wrong" in a COVID-19 World

When I started writing this book, we (the truly global "we"), were just starting to hear rumblings about a new kind of respiratory illness causing unexpected numbers of deaths in a few countries. A month later, the entire world knew about the novel coronavirus, and the illness that it causes, COVID-19. A few weeks after that, businesses and schools closed down, hundreds of thousands of people had died, the world was in the grip of a pandemic, entire countries were locked down, and unemployment rates rose to unprecedented highs.

Young adults like you, just starting to live an independent adult life, had to put their plans on hold. Dream jobs vanished as companies went bankrupt. Internships were cancelled. College graduations happened virtually, if at all. Many young adults moved back home with their parents, for reasons ranging from financial insecurity to needing to be part of and closer to a support network.

For you, COVID-19 may have put your launch into full-fledged adulting on hold. Or, it may have accelerated it, as you became sick or a caregiver to someone who was, and had to deal with the very adult decisions and fears that come with that.

Without a doubt, though, this pandemic has redefined everyone's definition of what can go wrong. I mean, this was definitely not something I ever expected to add to this chapter!

That said, even in the midst of a pandemic, you are still facing other adult challenges and other things that may go wrong. And you need to know what to do then, too.

Let's talk about some of these situations, what you can do to be proactive, and what you can do to be reactive. These aren't in ranked order from big to small, because it doesn't matter whether what you're dealing with is big or small. It's real, and it can be scary to realize it's up to you to fix or deal with it. Like in a pit-in-your-stomach, throat-clenched-up, can't-breathe kind of scary.

What to Have on Hand for Basic Home Repair

With the right tools and YouTube, you'll probably be able to tackle most of your own basic home repairs. Just don't be like me and realize you don't have a basic tool kit on hand the night before you're putting together the amazing new Big Wheel you bought your nephew to be aunt of the year. (Side note: A high-heeled shoe may serve as a hammer in a pinch, but don't expect to wear that pair of heels ever again.) Be smarter and put together a tool kit to have on hand before something breaks or needs to be put together.

8 Basic Tools for Home Repair

1. Hammer. *See also:* Reference to high heels above. Seriously though, a small hammer is kind of a crucial tool. It's how you pound in nails to hang up pictures or that stick up just enough to snag your socks when you walk through the door frame.

2. Combination pliers. Combination pliers are sometimes also called side-cutting pliers, which is kind of a daunting name. What you need to know is these pliers are multipurpose. Because they have those wedged, teeth-like gripping jaws, they can be used to grip, twist, grab, and pull things. They also have a cutting edge to cut through wire or things like heavy-duty staples (the kind that come from staple guns).

3. Needle-nose pliers. Have you ever tried to fix the clasp of a piece of jewelry that came open? Or needed to pick up a tiny screw or other small object you dropped into a small crack in the floor? Those are two cases in which needle-nose pliers would serve you well. They can also be used to bend small-gauge wire, like the kind you use on Christmas ornaments.

4. Phillips-head screwdriver. It's frustrating to go to tighten (or loosen) a screw and realize the screw head is shaped like a little cross, not just one slot. That's why you need a Phillips-head screwdriver. You may want to buy a set of them in various sizes.

5. Flathead screwdriver. This is the screwdriver that you've been using a butter knife to replace. The butter knife may work, but the flathead screwdriver gives you better leverage and will probably cause you to swear less. Again, you may want to invest in a set of them in various sizes.

6. Tape measure. I already mentioned I have no sense of direction. I also have no sense of space. When someone says to me, "You need to be six feet apart," it means absolutely nothing to me. So, I bought one of those easy-lock tape measures. Now I can not only measure out six feet, but I can also lock the tape measure in place, so I see it for more than just a quick second. It's also a great way to measure to make sure furniture will fit.

7. Utility knife or box cutter. I mean, how else are you going to cut through the tape on your Amazon boxes? Or, you know, cut a straight, precise line; trim excess wallpaper; cut through cardboard; or cut packing or duct tape.

8. Level. I'm more inclined to use a leveling app on my smart phone, but a true level really works better. If you're someone who wants your pictures to be absolutely straight or needs to make sure your washing machine is level so it stops rattling and vibrating, invest in a level.

WHAT YOU NEED TO KNOW ABOUT FIRE EXTINGUISHERS

OK, so as an adult, the first thing you need to know about a fire extinguisher is that you should have one in your home and have it handy. Then, you need to know how to use it, and not so you can recreate the scene of any movie in which people spray them at people in self-defense. The truth is you never know when the oil you're frying donuts in is going to drip onto the burner and catch on fire. (That's a true story. It was terrifying.)

Before you get to even using the fire extinguisher, make sure you know the different classifications of fires, and make sure you have the right type of extinguisher to deal with it. All fire extinguishers are labeled to show which classes of fire they can fight. Most home fire extinguishers are multipurpose for different kinds of fires (see the chart on the next page).

Types of Fires and Extinguishers

Fire Extinguisher Type (Label color)	WATER (Red)	FOAM (Gray)	POWDER (Blue)	CO2 (Black)	WET CHEMICAL (Yellow)
Wood, paper, and cloth	✔	✔	✔	✗	✔
Flammable liquids: gasoline, grease, paint, and solvents	✗	✔	✔	✔	✗
Live electrical equipment: computers	✗	✗	✔	✗	✗
Electrical contact	✗	✗	✔	✔	✗
Kitchen fires: cooking oil, vegetable oil	✗	✗	✗	✗	✔

Using a Fire Extinguisher

1 | First, know your escape route.

Using a fire extinguisher will either put out a small fire or give you an opportunity to get out of there so the fire department can take over. Identify your nearest exit, so you know which way to go once you discharge the fire extinguisher.

2 | Stand with your back to the exit.

As scary as it sounds, you'll have to face the fire. Move about six feet away from the fire with your back to the identified exit. (If you're like me and can't tell what six feet is, just back waaay up.)

3 | Remember to use the acronym PASS.

Just like "stop, drop, and roll," there's another catchy fire safety way to remember what to do. PASS stands for:

- **P**ull the pin.
- **A**im the nozzle. (Aim at the bottom of the fire to put it out.)
- **S**queeze the trigger.
- **S**weep from side to side. (Basically, swing the nozzle from side to side for the not quite thirty seconds of discharge time.)

CREATING AN EMERGENCY DISASTER PLAN

Disasters happen. That's what makes them disasters, not planned disruptions. Having a plan to deal with house fires, wildfires, earthquakes, tornados, floods, hurricanes, blizzards, pandemics, or other national emergencies is critical. It's especially important if you don't live near or with family. It's one of the reasons I mentioned earlier that you should put an ICE (in case of emergency) contact in your phone.

Know What Could Happen and What You'll Need

If you live in California, it's more likely you need a plan in case of earthquakes or wildfires than for blizzards. Know what types of natural disasters occur in your area in order to be best prepared.

Make a Disaster Supply Kit or "To-Go" Bag

Basically, this is a grab-and-go bag you have packed and ready so you can evacuate quickly. Some people pack them in duffle bags and have them near their door. In our house, we use a plastic tote, not only because it's waterproof, but also because we have to pack for a whole family. It keeps everything in one place and is portable. You don't need to pack up your whole place—just enough items to survive about three days if you have to leave your home. The United States Department of Homeland Security recommends that you include:

- Water
- Nonperishable food
- A first-aid kit
- A week's worth of prescription medications (if you can)
- Important documents, like insurance policies, passports, and your medical information in a waterproof container. If you can't keep them all in one place, consider taking photos or scans and uploading them to cloud storage or putting them on an external drive that you can put in your emergency kit.
- A contact list of your family members and other people in your support network. (Act as if you won't have your phone with you and will need all of their info accessible in some other way.)
- Some cash in case ATMs and card readers are down because of power outages
- A flashlight and batteries, and, if possible, a hand-crank or battery-powered radio
- Matches in a waterproof container
- A cell phone charger and maybe a power pack

Know Where You're Going

Shelters and safe places will vary by emergency, and you need to figure out the safe spaces in your home and at least one outside of it. For instance, know where you can shelter-in-place if there's a tornado or earthquake.

Know where your local shelter is and at least two routes to get there. That's the place to head to if you need to leave your home. It's also the place where most people will try to find each other if they're separated from or worried about friends and family.

Know How You'll Communicate

Being an adult means you're going to need to let people know where you are and how you're doing in an emergency. Don't wait until there is one to figure out how to get in touch with people. It's worth having the conversation ahead of time. Are you going to call people? Text them? Meet them? Check in on Facebook? If you have a large family-and-friends network, you may even want to create a call tree in which people have designated people to check in on and a way to pass that information on to everyone else.

SOME BASIC SELF-DEFENSE

It's not comfortable to think about, but sometimes what goes wrong is a matter of personal safety. Keeping yourself safe matters, and being able to defend yourself against an attack is something everyone should know how to do. I'd highly recommend taking a self-defense and safety course if you can, so that you can practice and learn techniques that will work for you. But in the meantime, here are some basic tips for when you can't get away.

Stay Alert and Look Confident

I want to be clear, even if you're not alert and confident, that doesn't mean it's your fault if you're attacked. We all get distracted and nervous, especially in places we don't know. The art of keeping my eyes up, paying attention to how close other people are to me, and walking as if I know exactly where I'm going is something I've had to learn over the years.

Throw a Tantrum

In the off chance you get grabbed from behind by an attacker, your best move is to throw a toddler tantrum. It's not just screaming and yelling, it's also about how you move your body. You know how toddlers go totally limp when you're trying to get them into a car seat or to move out of your way? (Dogs do this, too.) If you get grabbed from behind, drop your weight, and move wildly from side to side so you're hard to hold onto. And like any self-respecting toddler, make sure to kick in the groin or shin for good measure.

Aim for the Soft Parts

This makes tons of sense to me. If you're going to fight back, you don't want to hurt yourself while you're doing it. Aiming for the chest, legs, fists, and so forth means you may hurt yourself. If you can't get away, try to throw your elbows, knees, or fists into an attacker's eyes, groin, and nose. And again, if you've been taken by surprise from behind, use your best toddler move—bump your head back hard into the person's nose and lips.

Additional Advice

- **Keep your phone in your bag or a front pocket.** When you're out walking or jogging, it keeps you from checking email or messages when you should be paying attention to what's happening around you.

- **Be clear about your boundaries.** Sometimes self-defense is against people you know. If you're not comfortable with their words or actions toward you, tell them so. Do it firmly and don't make those boundaries negotiable.
- **Invest in ambient-sound earbuds.** Getting lost in your music while you run or walk may seem great, but it's not a great way to keep track of what's happening around you. Invest in a pair of ear buds that still allow you to hear what's going on around you, whether that's traffic or a person coming up on you.
- **Trust your gut.** A friend who is a neuropsychologist pointed out to me that that feeling you get sometimes that something's not right is a biological instinct. She said pay attention to it because it's better to have oversensitive instincts than to be attacked. I think she has an excellent point.

THINGS YOU NEVER THOUGHT TO THINK ABOUT

There are things you think might go wrong, and then there are things that go wrong you haven't really stopped to think about. For most adults, even if those things are little, they can be paralyzing. Because seriously, I totally thought about what to do in the case of an earthquake, but it never occurred to me I'd be standing in a hotel room by myself trying to contort to manage the back zipper of the only fancy dress I brought with me for a night out. There are too many things that may go wrong for me to list here, but here are a few that have come up not only for me, but also for other actual adults I know.

How Do You Sew on a Button?

At the very least, have a basic sewing kit that includes needles, different colors of thread, and a basic scissors. You can usually pick one of these up at the grocery or drugstore.

1 | Thread a needle with about two feet of thread.

Making sure you have thread that matches your garment, you should have an equal length of about one foot on either side of the eye of the needle. Knot both ends of the thread together, so that you have a double layer of thread.

2 | Position your button in the right place.

Check to make sure the buttonholes will match up with the button.

3 | Start sewing.

Hold the button in place and push the threaded needle up through the bottom of the fabric through one of the holes in the button. Pull until the knot hits the fabric. If you have a two-hole button, push the needle down through the hole that it didn't come up through, and then up through the first hole, down through the second, several times. If you have a four-hole button, push the needle down through the hole diagonally across from where it came through. Push up through one of the holes next to it and then back down through the hole diagonally across from that one. Repeat this until you have made an X with the thread. Make that X twice more to make sure the button is securely on.

4 | Finish.

Push the needle up under the button (but not up through a hole), and loop the thread around where the button is sewed to the fabric. Do this twice, push the needle down under the button to the back of the fabric, tie it off in a knot and cut off the remaining thread.

How Do You Zip Up a Fancy Dress When You Live by Yourself?

This is actually not as hard as it seems, especially if your dress has a zipper pull with a hole in it. Grab a shoelace or a length of ribbon that reaches from your neck to the small of your back. Tie it to a heavy-duty safety pin or paper clip. Slip the safety pin or paper clip through the hole in the zipper pull. Zip up as far as you can and then use the ribbon or shoelace to pull it up the rest of the way.

If the pull doesn't have a hole in it, you can tie the shoelace or ribbon to a clothespin or binder clip. Clamp the zipper pull in the teeth of the clothespin and zip up the same way.

What If You Can't Find Your Keys and You're Going to Be Late for Work?

Don't panic! Losing keys has happened to all of us, and for some reason it never seems to happen when you don't need to get somewhere. First, call your boss, and let them know you're running late. Then, take a few deep breaths, stop tearing the house apart, and think more logically. Check the pockets of your coat. Look in the front door to see if you left your keys there when you came in the day before. Put on your shoes and look in your car to make sure you didn't lock them in. (It's unlikely if you needed them to get in your door, too.) Look in the most unlikely places—your fridge, the bathroom, and under the couch.

Then, do a quick time check. If you're not going to be able to find them and get to work at a reasonable time, make a decision: Take public transportation, get a ride to work, or take the day off to search for your keys. Just make sure you keep your boss updated.

What Do You Do If You Lose Your Job?

Even if you hate your job, no longer having the security of a steady paycheck can be unnerving to say the least. And even though lots of people lose jobs through no fault of their own, others may jump to the conclusion that you did something to get fired. So, one of the first things you may want to do is think through how to communicate your job loss.

There's a difference between saying, "I lost my job," "I was laid off," "My company just cut 20% of its staff," "The place I worked at had to close," and "I got fired." Think through what it is you want or need people to know in order to feel supported, and create a communication plan. Then start telling people. You never know who knows of an open job in your field. I know a couple of people who had interviews within a day of losing a job because they told people right away, and those people knew of something else that was a good fit.

Next, file for unemployment in your state. You should qualify if you lost your job through no fault of your own, and in some cases, even if you were fired. There may be a waiting period, and you'll have to actively job hunt, but it gives you income while you search.

Evaluate and take a look at your budget. Do you have savings? Are you going to struggle to pay your rent? If you're going to have trouble paying your rent in full, and there's nobody who can help you out temporarily, talk to your landlord about your options.

Lastly, know that it may take some time to find a perfect new job. Depending on your financial situation, you may have to take a not-so-desirable job to make it through while you look.

A Few Last Thoughts on Adulting

You are coming into adulthood in a time of tremendous change. You've inherited a world filled with pandemics, climate change, and economic uncertainty. But you've also developed resilience and are part of a generation of change-makers and doers. The details of being an adult may be new to you, but creative ideas and innovative thinking aren't. You're going to be an awesome adult, and the world is going to be a better place for it. Happy adulting!

INDEX

ACKNOWLEDGMENTS

Writing a book is lots of work, not just for the author, but for the people who live with them. I want to thank my husband, Jon, for so many things. For letting me tell not-always-flattering anecdotes about you. For taking on more than your fair share of adulting while I wrote this book. For listening to chapter after chapter read out loud, and for telling me when I wasn't nearly as funny as I thought I was. I love you, and there's nobody I'd rather muddle through adulthood with.

To my chronologically adult children, Megan and Jacob: You're my favorite test cases, and though I know how much I annoy you, it just means I love you enough to want you to leave my house—as successful adults, of course. And to Benjamin, the one who is still left, I promise I love you enough to want you to leave, too.

I'm so grateful to all my friends and co-workers who shared stories of adulting fails, challenges, and wins. You all graciously handed me ideas of things I never would have considered to add to this book and let me take credit for them. That's true friendship.

Thanks to Pam Wissman, editor extraordinaire for your insight, eye to detail, appreciation of my quirky sense of humor, and grace in answering emails filled with out-of-the-blue questions tinged with panic. You're not only a great editor, you're a great friend. Thanks to Celia, for her gut check and advice to go easy on myself when looking back on my early adulting failures.

Lastly, thank you to SoHo Publishing and Mixed Media Resources for the opportunity to write this book, as well as art director Irene Ledwith, designer Danita Albert, and the Sterling sales team.